Marian Cox

Cambridge IGCSE®
First Language English

Coursebook

Fourth Edition

CAMBRIDGE
UNIVERSITY PRESS

CAMBRIDGE
UNIVERSITY PRESS

University Printing House, Cambridge CB2 8BS, United Kingdom

It furthers the University's mission by disseminating knowledge in the pursuit of education, learning and research at the highest international levels of excellence.

Information on this title: education.cambridge.org

© Cambridge University Press 2002, 2010, 2014

First published 2002
Second edition 2006
Third edition 2010
Fourth edition 2014
3rd printing 2015

Printed by Multivista Global Ltd, India

ISBN 978-1-107-65782-3 Paperback

Additional resources for this publication at education.cambridge.org

The publisher is grateful to the following expert reviewers:
Mair Lewis, Tony Parkinson.

....

Contents

Introduction   v

Skills grid   vii

Part 1: Travel and sport   1

Unit 1   Reading Comprehension: skimming and scanning, selecting points for summary, making notes using your own words, looking at writers' language choices   1

Unit 2   Response Writing: journals, letters, considering audience, choosing a style   10

Unit 3   Continuous Writing: (Descriptive) planning compositions, writing descriptions, using adjectives and imagery   20

Part 2: Work and education   31

Unit 4   Reading Comprehension: understanding, selecting and organising material for summary questions   31

Unit 5   Response Writing: transforming information, news reports, letters   42

Unit 6   Continuous Writing: (Informative and descriptive) giving an account, structuring description   51

Part 3: People and society   58

Unit 7   Reading Comprehension: expanding notes, sentence structure, vocabulary building, summary style, analysing how writers achieve effects   58

Unit 8   Response to Reading: persuasive devices, analysing techniques, writing publicity material, drawing inferences, writing in role, targeting an audience   67

Unit 9   Continuous Writing: (Narrative) plot, setting and atmosphere   82

Part 4: Ideas and technology   93

Unit 10   Reading Comprehension: collating texts, analysing style, vocabulary building, advanced punctuation   93

Unit 11   Response Writing: spelling techniques, expressing and supporting a view, collating and ordering information, reports and articles   106

Unit 12   Continuous Writing: (Narrative) character, voice, viewpoint, using dialogue   118

iii

Part 5: Speaking and listening 127

Unit 13 Giving a talk and conducting a dialogue: preparing a talk; answering questions, engaging in dialogue 127

Unit 14 Group discussion and making a speech: facts versus opinions, defending opinions, delivering a speech 138

List of terms 149

Acknowledgements 151

Introduction

The Cambridge IGCSE First Language English syllabus is designed as a two-year course for examination at age 16+ for students whose English is of native, near-native or bilingual standard. It offers a wide, relevant and accessible curriculum tailored to international needs and an assessment scheme which rewards positive achievement. First Language English is accepted as a UK higher education entrance requirement equivalent to the same grade at GCSE or to IELTS 6.5, and is recognised as a suitable foundation for A Level, IB and Pre-U certificate studies.

This coursebook covers the whole Cambridge IGCSE First Language English syllabus and curriculum and contains enough material for a five-term programme of study. Each of the 14 units has a rich variety of activities and tasks sufficient to last for several weeks of classroom lessons plus homework. Teachers may wish to be selective in the setting of tasks in order to target the particular needs of students, but each of the first 12 units is relevant to examinations, whichever component options have been selected. Each unit ends with three extension activities or further practice tasks for students to do at home. Answers to the coursebook activities are available to teachers online at education.cambridge.org

Key points and Task tips occur frequently in each unit: Key points give guidance on essential skills, syllabus requirements and exam technique; Task tips offer explanations and support for responding to the specific tasks. All the experience and advice needed for students to perform at the highest level in English language examinations is provided.

Students are advised to work through the units in sequence; as the learning support and skills development are progressive, and there is specific teaching of sentence building, vocabulary extension, punctuation and spelling. The emphasis is on the acquisition and application of transferable skills, with a mixture of preparatory and exam-type tasks in every unit. There is revisiting and reinforcement of skills across the units, and the basic and generic skills of selecting, planning, checking, paraphrasing and note-taking occur throughout. A skills grid indicates the main focus of the activities in each unit and where they could be used for Speaking and Listening assessment.

The coursebook supports students studying for both core and extended level examination tiers. The Response Writing units build skills and provide practice in content, structure and style for written responses in papers based on reading passages, which include directed writing and an evaluation of ideas contained in a text. The Continuous Writing units focus on the skills needed for the narrative and descriptive choices in composition papers and coursework. They contain suggestions for possible coursework assignment topics, provide texts that contain facts, opinions and arguments for analysis and evaluation, and offer a variety of stimulus resources for composition writing.

Speaking and Listening skills are covered in the book, with numerous opportunities for the skills acquisition and classroom practice of aural and oral activities in a variety of groupings and situations; to help students prepare for Speaking and Listening examinations or coursework. In addition, there are two units at the end of the book (in Part 5) that focus specifically on speaking and listening, which also give further opportunity for reading and writing skills development.

The book is divided into four themed sections: Travel and sport, Work and education, People and society, and Ideas and technology. Each section is sub-divided into units corresponding to three key assessment areas: Reading Comprehension, Response Writing and Continuous Writing. The themes were chosen for their international applicability and relevance, variety and intrinsic interest to students. The majority of texts are authentic and recent, and they are an enriching mixture of those encountered in everyday life and those typical of the types of passage students may encounter in an exam. The coursebook draws upon a wide variety of sources, genres, registers and issues, and has been designed to be user-friendly as well as academically stimulating.

By the end of the coursebook students should have become more confident in thinking about language, handling and responding to texts, and approaching and fulfilling tasks. They should also have expanded their vocabulary, increased their accuracy and improved in all the skills areas; so that they are fully prepared to sit exams successfully, and to transfer their language skills to further education and to the workplace.

The other components of this IGCSE suite, by the same author, are:

■ an interactive e-book version of the coursebook
■ a skill-building student Workbook
■ a Teacher's Resource Book
■ online resources.

Skills grid

	Unit 1	Unit 2	Unit 3	Unit 4	Unit 5	Unit 6	Unit 7
READING							
response to reading							
comprehension	✓						
vocabulary extension	✓	✓		✓	✓		
inference	✓	✓		✓	✓		
prediction					✓		
comparison						✓	
writer's effects							
explaining meanings							✓
explaining effects	✓	✓				✓	
connotations					✓		✓
images				✓	✓		
style analysis							
summary					✓		
identifying points					✓	✓	✓
paraphrasing	✓				✓		
concision/connectives				✓			✓
WRITING							
directed writing							
evaluating		✓					
refuting							
persuasive language					✓		
collating		✓					
sequencing		✓			✓		
register/style							
spelling							
punctuation	✓						
description							
adjectives			✓		✓		
figurative language			✓				
framework			✓			✓	
style			✓			✓	
openings/endings			✓				
narrative							
plot/pace							
character							
setting/atmosphere							
voice/viewpoint							
narrative dialogue							
openings/endings			✓				
argument							
discursive							
persuasive							
informative			✓				
structuring discourse			✓				
rhetorical devices							
SPEAKING/LISTENING							
giving a talk							
responding to a talk							
choosing register							
dialogue							
interview				✓			
delivering a speech							
assessing a speech							
scripting a speech							
using rhetoric							
paired argument							
roleplay							
recognising bias							
group discussion				✓			

	Unit 8	Unit 9	Unit 10	Unit 11	Unit 12	Unit 13	Unit 14
READING							
response to reading							
comprehension							
vocabulary extension			✓				
inference	✓		✓				
prediction							
comparison	✓		✓				
writer's effects							
explaining meanings			✓				
explaining effects	✓		✓				
connotations	✓	✓	✓				
images			✓				
style analysis	✓		✓				
summary							
identifying points	✓		✓				
paraphrasing			✓	✓			
concision/connectives							
WRITING							
directed writing							
evaluating				✓			✓
refuting	✓			✓			✓
persuasive language	✓			✓			
collating			✓	✓			
sequencing	✓			✓			
register/style				✓			
spelling				✓			
punctuation			✓	✓	✓		
description							
adjectives		✓					
figurative language							
framework		✓					
style							
openings/endings					✓		
narrative							
plot/pace		✓					
character					✓		
setting/atmosphere		✓					
voice/viewpoint		✓			✓		
narrative dialogue					✓		
openings/endings		✓			✓		
argument							
discursive							
persuasive							
informative							
structuring discourse				✓			
rhetorical devices				✓			
SPEAKING/LISTENING							
giving a talk						✓	
responding to a talk						✓	
choosing register						✓	
dialogue						✓	
interview						✓	
delivering a speech	✓						✓
assessing a speech							✓
scripting a speech							✓
using rhetoric							✓
paired argument	✓						✓
roleplay							✓
recognising bias			✓	✓			✓
group discussion	✓	✓			✓		✓

Part 1:
Travel and sport

Unit 1: Reading Comprehension

This unit focuses on reading for gist and for specific information, on the selection of key points for summary, and on writers' choice of language.

1   You are going to read a passage about an island. To get you in the mood, with your partner jot down words associated with islands. Create a **mind map** to connect all the ideas that you can think of.

2   Looking at your mind map, think about possible answers to the following questions and contribute to class discussion:

   a   Which islands or types of island are you imagining?

   b   Why are islands generally considered attractive?

   c   What are the disadvantages of living on or being on an island?

3   Skim-read the passage below, which is an **informative** piece about the island of Tenerife.

KEY POINT

A summary is a reduced version of a text and its aim is informative. When you **summarise** a passage, you need to identify the key words in the text (single words or **phrases** which tell you what each part of the text is about). It is useful to have a highlighter with you in an exam so that you can annotate the reading passage to select material for any summary questions. Highlight only the essential points rather than whole sentences or paragraphs.

These are the parts of a passage **not** to use in your response to Activity 6: repetitions, minor details, quotations or **direct speech**, **imagery**, examples, lists.

KEY POINT

Paragraphing is a logical way of dividing text. Paragraphs usually consist of several sentences which group similar information together. A break between paragraphs shows a change of topic, time or place. As well as being necessary for structuring text, paragraphs are a courtesy to the reader to aid their understanding.

❝ VOCABULARY

archipelago: group of islands

---

4 Without looking at the passage, answer the following general questions on Tenerife. Compare your answers with those of a partner, then check the passage to see who is right.

  a What are the most noticeable features of the scenery?

  b What can tourists spend their time doing?

  c What is the temperature like?

  d What contributes to the economy?

  e What is there to see?

5 Scan the passage and find the single word in each paragraph which could be used as a topic heading for that paragraph. Are your choices the same as your partner's?

Taking a trip round
Tenerife

The Spanish island of Tenerife lies about 300 km off the West African coast, and is the largest, most populous and most productive of the seven Canary Islands, believed to be named after the ferocious dogs (*canaria*) found there by early explorers. Santa Cruz is its capital, and the shared capital (with Las Palmas) of the whole **archipelago**.

This rugged, rocky and steep island looks up to El Teide, the third largest volcano in the world and the highest point in Spain at 3718 m. Its often snow-covered peak gave the island its name, which means 'white mountain'. Ravines and valleys are another striking feature of the island's terrain, some of them formed by volcanic eruptions, four of which were recorded between 1704 and 1909. The island has 342 km of coastline and boasts nearly 70 km of beach, the ones on the northern coast consisting of black sand rather than the lighter, finer sand of the south. The island has two distinct landscapes and atmospheres: the lush, green north and the barren, developed south.

Tenerife is known as the 'Island of Eternal Spring'; since it is on the same latitude as the Sahara Desert, it enjoys a warm climate and plenty of sunshine all year round. However, the trade winds create cloud and cold sea currents, keeping temperatures moderate, with an average of 13–18 °C in the winter and 24–28 °C in the summer.

The Canaries are one of the major tourist destinations in the world and tourism is Tenerife's main industry, with about five million visitors each year using one of its two airports. There are two main highways crossing the island, as well as dizzying narrow mountain roads in the north. Tourists mainly visit the south of the island, which is hotter and drier and has many resorts, such as Playa de las Americas and Los Cristianos. The only new hotels

6   With a partner, in pencil or on a copy of the passage put brackets around the material you would **not** use in a summary about the island.

7   Skim the passage below about Cape Town, and decide where it should be divided into paragraphs.

8   How many paragraphs did you make? Compare and discuss with your partner why you would put breaks in the places you chose.

9   Scan the passage and for each of the paragraphs think of a heading to indicate its topic, as if for a tourist **brochure**. This time, instead of using words from the passage, think of **synonyms** (words or phrases with the same meaning) where possible.

permitted to be built must be of 5-star quality to promote environmentally conscious development.

The area known as Costa Adeje has many world-class facilities and leisure activities to offer besides sea and sand, such as quality shopping centres, golf courses, restaurants, waterparks, animal parks and a theatre. In February, visitors can enjoy one of the world's largest carnivals. The distinctive local craft is Tenerife lace – the embroidery of stretched cloth for table linen – which visitors can see being made. Wildlife attractions are the UNESCO Biosphere Reserve, opened in 2013, the botanical gardens in Puerto de la Cruz and a butterfly park in Icod de los Vinos.

Agriculture contributes only 10% to the island's economy but it supports the landscape and the cultural values of the island. In the coastal areas, tomatoes and bananas are cultivated, and these are exported to mainland Spain and the rest of Europe. At lower and drier altitudes, potatoes, tobacco and maize are the most common crops. Grapes are grown on steep north-facing slopes and onions in the south. Flowers are also produced for the export market. The islands are important to Spain as fishing grounds.

Tenerife has several archaeological sites, consisting mainly of the cave paintings prevalent in the south. Also noteworthy are the buildings called Güímar Pyramids, whose origin is uncertain, and the defensive castles located in the village of San Andrés and elsewhere on the island. There are many other interesting historical buildings, such as the Convent of San Augustin and the Church of San Marcos. Other impressive but more modern structures are the Auditorio de Tenerife, at the entry port to the capital, and the Torres de Santa Cruz, a skyscraper 120 metres high.

There are pretty hill towns to look around, and from one of them, Masca, one can set off on the famous hike down the gorge. This is full of rich vegetation, large and colourful plants, and a range of animal species. Garachico is a small, unspoilt fishing town whose quiet streets are dotted with bars, cafés and gift shops, and there are some superb fish restaurants down by the harbour. Sight-seeing in the nearby smaller town of Icod de los Vinos must include the island's most prized possession, the Dragon Tree, which stands in a preserved garden and is said to be approximately 1000 years old.

10 Summarise in one sentence the attractions Cape Town has for visitors, according to the passage.

CᵃPE TᵒWN

With its majestic Table Mountain backdrop, Cape Town is one of the most beautiful cities in the world. A harmonious blend of architectural styles reflects the tastes of the past as well as today's more functional requirements. Between the high-rise office blocks, Edwardian and Victorian buildings have been meticulously preserved, and many outstanding examples of Cape Dutch architecture are found. Narrow, cobblestone streets and the strongly Islamic presence of the Bo-Kaap enhance the cosmopolitan ambiance of the city. Cape Town's shopping options invite you to endlessly browse. Elegant malls such as the Victoria Wharf at the V & A Waterfront, antique shops, craft markets, flea markets and art galleries abound. Specialist boutiques offer an enticing array of unusual items not readily obtainable elsewhere. One of Cape Town's biggest tourist attractions, the Waterfront, **evokes** images of the early activities of the harbour. Much of its charm lies in the fact that this busy commercial harbour is set in the midst of a huge entertainment venue with pubs, restaurants, shops, craft markets, theatres and movies. Table Mountain is undeniably the biggest tourist attraction in South Africa, drawing local holidaymakers as well as tourists from the four corners of the globe. The summit can be reached by trails or cable-car, but mountaineers do it the hard way. On a clear day, the spectacular views from the summit (1086 metres above sea level) stretch across the mountainous spine of the Cape Peninsula and beyond Table Bay and Robben Island. Robben Island, which lies about 11 kilometres north of Cape Town, has over the years become synonymous with the anti-apartheid struggle in South Africa. It was here that activists such as Nelson Mandela and Walter Sisulu, among many others, were imprisoned because of their opposition to apartheid. The historical importance of Robben Island (meaning 'Seal Island') can be gauged by its designation as a cultural heritage site. Stretching away from Table Bay Harbour, the Atlantic seafront features virgin beaches along undeveloped frontages to the north, and densely populated Sea Point to the south, leading on to the Clifton, Camps Bay and Llandudno beauty spots, among others. The western coastline is characterised by rocky outcrops and beautiful beaches. Major national and international windsurfing competitions are held at Bloubergstrand. Seal-watching is an amusing diversion. Boat trips around the harbour and along the coast are always popular.

Adapted from **www.sa-venues.com**

Day 56 – Luxor

11 Read the passage below, which is about a stop in Egypt during a journey from the North Pole to the South Pole without using air transport.

At 5.35 in the morning the train pulls into Luxor, known by the Greeks as Thebes, 420 miles south of Cairo, in Upper Egypt. I cannot conceal my excitement at being here for the first time in my life.

Luxor Station is tastefully <u>monumental</u> in decoration, with tall columns, gilded details on the doors, eagle heads and a <u>hieroglyphic</u> design somehow <u>incorporating</u> power stations, railways and ancient history. Figures materialise from the pre-dawn gloom to offer us taxi rides. You will never stand on your own for long in Egypt.

We shall be joining a Nile cruise for the next leg of our journey, and as we drive along the river to find our boat – the *Isis* – I can see ranks of chunky four-storeyed vessels, maybe 100 in all, lined up along the riverbank, awaiting the day the tourists come back.

My guide to Luxor is a tall, straight, matchstick-thin aristocrat of the business whose name is Tadorus but who asks me to call him Peter … 'It's easier.' I would rather call him Tadorus, but he doesn't look the sort you argue with. He is 83 years old, and as a boy of 14 was present when the archaeologist Howard Carter first pushed open the door of Tutankhamun's tomb.

Peter takes me across on the Nile ferry to a cluster of mud buildings on the West Bank opposite the city. We are driven past fields of sugar cane and alongside an irrigation canal financed by the Russians in 1960.

The greenery ends abruptly as we climb a winding road up into barren, rubble-strewn desert. Then we are into the Valley of the Kings, which resembles a gigantic quarry, littered with rock <u>debris</u>, bleached white by the sun. We leave the bus and walk up towards the tombs in dry and scorching heat. Peter estimates the temperature at 40° Celsius, 104° Fahrenheit.

This vast necropolis contains the remains of 62 Pharaohs of the New Kingdom, established in Thebes between 3000 and 3500 years ago. It was discovered – 'rediscovered', as Peter corrects me – in 1892. Only 40 of the tombs have been found, and all, bar one, had been emptied by robbers.

(Continued)

6

We walk down into the tomb of Rameses III. The walls are covered in rich paintings and complex inscriptions illustrating the progress of the Pharaoh on his journey through the underworld, filled with wicked serpents, crocodiles and other creatures waiting to <u>devour</u> him. Because of the dry desert air, they are well preserved, an extraordinary historical document.

The sun is setting behind the Valley of the Kings when we return on the ferry. At this indescribably beautiful time of day, when the rich golden brown of the lower sky spills onto the surface of the Nile, turning it an intense amber, and the palm trees along the bank glow for a few precious minutes in the reflection, it is not difficult to imagine the power and spectacle of a funeral procession bearing the God-King's body across this same river, three and a half thousand years ago, at the beginning of his last and most important journey.

Adapted from *Pole to Pole*, by Michael Palin, BBC Publishing, London, 1995.

KEY POINT

Try to **paraphrase** the information in texts when gathering points together, and to make your phrases shorter than those in the text (see the example in Activity 15). If you are not sure what a word means, it is safer not to change it, although you can still change other words in the phrase. Technical terms often do not have synonyms, or it would take too many words to paraphrase them (e.g. solar heating, irrigation canal).

KEY POINT

When working under timed conditions you probably won't have time to write a draft for your summary, so group and order your material before you begin to write. The best way to **structure** your response is by bracketing and numbering your list of points. Do not confuse a summary with a commentary: you are not required to present information in the same order as in the passage, or to give your views on the material.

TASK TIP

Rather than using one **simple sentence** for each point, try to combine material into longer and more complex sentences. Avoid beginning each sentence the same way or repeating the same structure (e.g. don't start every sentence with *He*) and avoid the overuse of *and*. Before you write each sentence, plan its structure in your head. Check your summary for omissions, repetitions and inaccuracies of fact.

12 **Five** words in the passage are underlined. Can you guess their meaning by looking at their **context** (the other words around them)? Use a dictionary to check your guesses, then write synonyms for the six words in your personal vocabulary list.

13 Which words and phrases in the passage best illustrate the appearance of:

    a the West Bank and the Valley of the Kings (paragraph 5)?

    b the tomb of Rameses III (paragraph 8)?

    c the Nile at sunset (paragraph 9)?

    For each of your choices, explain why they are effective.

14 Scan the passage for the information given about Luxor and identify the key phrases.

15 Make a grid as shown below and list the key phrases and your paraphrases.

Key phrase	Point
barren, rubble-strewn desert	*wasteland*

16 Use your answers to Activities **5** and **15** to summarise the characteristics of **a** Tenerife and **b** Luxor in about 100 words *in total*. Use one paragraph for each place.

17 As a class, discuss what you already know or think about the following topics:

    a Robinson Crusoe

    b desert islands

    c books, films or television series set on desert islands

    d survival techniques.

18 Read the text below about Robinson Crusoe, which is an extract from a novel written in 1719 that includes journal entries.

19 In one sentence, describe the situation of Robinson Crusoe on the Island of Despair by answering these questions in any order:

    ■ Who is he?

    ■ What happened to him?

    ■ When did it happen?

    ■ Where is he?

    ■ How did he get there?

20 You are going to write a summary of Robinson Crusoe's:

    ■ needs

    ■ difficulties

    ■ fears

    ■ disappointments.

    First, make brief notes under each heading. Then, write a one-paragraph summary, in modern English, using all your notes.

Robinson Crusoe

September 30, 1659.

I, poor miserable Robinson Crusoe, being shipwrecked, during a dreadful storm, came on shore on this dismal unfortunate island, which I called the Island of Despair, all the rest of the ship's company being drowned, and myself almost dead.

All the rest of that day I spent in afflicting myself at the dismal circumstances I was brought to, viz. I had neither food, house, clothes, weapon, or place to fly to; and in despair of any relief, saw nothing but death before me; either that I should be devoured by wild beasts, murdered by savages, or starved to death for want of food. At the approach of night, I slept in a tree for fear of wild creatures, but slept soundly, though it rained all night.

From the 1st of October to the 24th.

All these days entirely spent in many several voyages to get all I could out of the ship, which I brought on shore, every tide of flood, upon rafts. Much rain also in these days, though with some intervals of fair weather; but, it seems, this was the rainy season.

October 26.

I walked about the shore almost all day to find out a place to fix my habitation, greatly concerned to secure myself from an attack in the night, either from wild beasts or men. Towards night I fixed upon a proper place under a rock, and marked out a semicircle for my encampment, which I resolved to strengthen with a work, wall, or fortification …

The 31st.

in the morning, I went out into the island with my gun to see for some food, and discover the country; when I killed a she-goat, and her kid followed me home, which I afterwards killed also, because it would not feed.

November 1.

I set up my tent under a rock, and lay there for the first night, making it as large as I could, with stakes driven in to swing my hammock upon.

November 17.

This day I began to dig behind my tent into the rock. Note, three things I wanted exceedingly for this work, viz. a pick-axe, a shovel, and a wheelbarrow or basket; so I ceased my work, and began to consider how to supply that want and make me some tools. A spade was so absolutely necessary, that indeed I could do nothing effectually without it; but what kind of one to make, I knew not.

January 1.

Very hot still, but I went abroad early and late with my gun, and lay still in the middle of the day. This evening, going farther into the valleys which lay towards the centre of the island, I found there was plenty of goats, though exceeding shy, and hard to come at. However, I resolved to try if I could not bring my dog to hunt them down.

January 2.

Accordingly, the next day, I went out with my dog, and set him upon the goats; but I was mistaken, for they all faced about upon the dog; and he knew his danger too well, for he would not come near them.

January 3.

I began my fence or wall; which being still fearful of my being attacked by somebody, I resolved to make very thick and strong.

All this time I worked very hard, the rains hindering me many days, nay, sometimes weeks together; but I thought I should never be perfectly secure till this wall was finished. And it is scarce credible what inexpressible labour everything was done with, especially the bringing piles out of the woods, and driving them into the ground; for I made them much bigger than I need to have done.

In the next place, I was at a great loss for candle; so that as soon as ever it was dark, which was generally by seven o'clock, I was obliged to go to bed.

Adapted from *Robinson Crusoe*, by Daniel Defoe.

9

21 With your partner, list future incidents or problems which Robinson Crusoe may face later in the novel, based on evidence in the extract. Share and support your predictions with the rest of the class.

➕ Further practice

a You have become stranded on a desert island! Write a description of the imaginary island. Think about its landscape, climate, vegetation, wildlife, food and water sources. You can use information from the island passages in Activities **3** and **18** of this unit to give you ideas.

b List the main features of your home town or rural area. Use the list to write an information leaflet for tourists, using bullet points. Group the points, divide them into sections, and give a topic heading to each section (e.g. *Things to see*). The passage in Activity **7** will help you with ideas.

c From what you have read in this unit, would you rather visit Tenerife, Cape Town or Luxor? Write the reasons for your preference, using details from the texts.

KEY POINT

Reading papers usually ask candidates to select and comment on language from a passage which gives a particular impression to the reader. Select and quote a range of short phrases (usually not more than two or three words each), and make clear that you understand both their meaning and their effect. In Further practice Activity **c**, your reasons for preferring a destination should be linked to the descriptive phrases which make it seem attractive, and the response each one evokes in you as a reader.

Unit 2: Response Writing

This unit prepares for the response to reading / directed writing tasks by considering form, audience and style. It focuses on writing journal entries and letters.

KEY POINT

Directed writing, or response to reading, tasks are those which ask you to use material in a text in a specified way. You will be given instructions about the CAP (content, audience and purpose). They usually require modification of the structure and style of the original passage, so you need to change vocabulary, sentence structures and text structure, rather than simply listing points from the passage in the same order and using the same words.

1 Discuss the following questions in class:
  a How would you define 'extreme sports'?
  b What examples can you think of?
  c What kind of people participate in them?
  d What makes these sports attractive?
  e Which ones would you consider doing or refuse to do?

2 Read the following passage, which is a newspaper review of a **non-fiction** book about a historical Arctic tragedy.

THE BIG CHILL

Arctic explorers are a breed apart, inevitably drawn, it would seem, by tragedy and the poetry of a 'good end'. Consider Shackleton. Having narrowly survived the loss of his ship, the *Endurance*, when it was crushed by ice in the Weddell Sea, he later died aboard the *Quest*, another Antarctic no-hoper, in 1922. Scott, of course, perished ten years earlier just a few miles from his base camp, having failed by a whisker to be the first to reach the South Pole. Amundsen, who beat his rival by just a couple of days, went on to die in an Arctic air crash.

Good chaps, each and every one of them. But what was it all about? In *The Ice Master*, an appropriately chilling account of the voyage of the *Karluk*, lead-ship of a doomed Arctic expedition in 1913–14, the motivation of those taking part seems to have been foolhardy at best. Vilhjalmur Stefansson, a Canadian of Nordic extraction, was an anthropologist and ethnologist who, for reasons best known to himself, believed that under the Arctic ice there lay a Lost Continent, a kind of wintry Atlantis, the discovery of which would make him famous. In reality, of course, there is no missing landmass; the Arctic Ocean is just what its name implies. But to the impatient Stefansson, the fact that there was, literally, no solid ground for his belief was defeatist talk.

Hiring a steely skipper, Captain Bob Bartlett, Stefansson ordered the *Karluk* to sea from Victoria in British Columbia on June 17th 1913. Few of his men had real Arctic experience. The 'scientists' on board knew very little of the trials ahead. The ship itself was a retired whaler, made of wood, staggeringly unsuited to its new purpose.

The crew, it transpires, had an eerie premonition of their fate. Stuck fast in the Alaskan floes, they were 'transfixed' by the diaries of George Washington De Long, another of their breed, who had died, along with all his men, in 1881. De Long's ship, the *Jeanette*, had been crushed by ice in almost exactly the same reach of the Arctic Ocean as the *Karluk*. One hundred and forty days passed before cold and starvation claimed the last of the expedition's victims.

Jennifer Niven, formerly a screenwriter, assembles her characters with all the skill of an experienced novelist. Both of the principals are carefully drawn. There is Bartlett, an energetic, skilful mariner, big in every way, with a booming voice and a love for literature and women. Stefansson, by contrast, comes across as an egotist of monstrous proportions. Charming, silver-tongued and handsome, he cared little for those under his command.

Locked together on the diminutive ship, the crew of the *Karluk* watched and listened in horror as the frozen sea closed in around them. The staff and officers gathered nightly in the saloon for Victrola concerts, choosing from among more than 200 records. As the gloom grew ever deeper, the lure of the library, with its terrible account of the fate of the *Jeanette*, increased by the day.

Stefansson cracked first. Loading up a dog-sledge, he and several others headed off into the night, ostensibly to hunt for food. Others would go to pieces later. Matters came to a head on January 10th when, with a thunderous roar, the ice broke through the ship's hull, forcing the captain to give the order to abandon ship.

In all, 16 men were to die, but Bartlett emerged as the true hero of the hour. Niven's account – always alive to the nuances of human strength as well as weakness – is at its strongest as she recounts his ghastly journey through the Arctic winter in search of help, and his equally determined quest for his lost crewmen when he at last found sanctuary in Siberia. Those who survived long enough for him to find them numbered a lucky 13, including two Eskimo girls and one of the scientists, McKinlay, who ever after regarded his captain as 'honest, fearless, reliable, loyal, everything a man should be'.

Stefansson, needless to say, survived as well. Having spectacularly betrayed his comrades, he went on to map and discover several Arctic islands. Collecting a medal for his achievements, he made no mention of the *Karluk*, its crew or the men who were lost.

Adapted from an article by Walter Ellis, *The Sunday Times*, 19th November 2000.

11

3 Discuss the following questions as a class:

a Why do you think book reviews are published in newspapers?

b Who do you think writes them, and why?

c Who do you think reads them, and why?

d Who do you think benefits from the reviews, and how?

e Who do you think would be interested in reading *The Ice Master*?

4 Publishers promote their new books by printing **blurbs** (brief descriptions of the type and content of the book) on their back covers. It is a rule that a blurb must not reveal what happens in the end, as this would deter readers. Write a blurb for *The Ice Master*, using three short paragraphs. You aim is to appeal to your audience and persuade them to buy the book:

■ Refer to the background of the expedition and its participants.

■ Describe the crisis situation the book deals with.

■ Refer to specific incidents which make the book sound exciting.

5 Find all the dates and time references in the article. Then list the events in **chronological** order (the order in which they occurred), together with their date or duration, in a grid like the one shown below. This will give you a sense of the overall time scheme, which will help you later. An example has been given.

Event	Time
The Jeanette crushed	1881

6 Read the following extracts from the journal of the Antarctic explorer Robert Falcon Scott (who is mentioned in the article in Activity **2**). On 16th January 1912, he discovered that the Norwegian explorer Roald Amundsen had beaten him to the South Pole.

17th Jan: Great God! This is an awful place and terrible enough for us to have laboured to it without the reward of priority. Well, it is something to have got here, and the wind may be our friend tomorrow.

18th Jan: Well, we have turned our back now on the goal of our ambition with sore feelings and must face 800 miles of solid dragging – and goodbye to the daydreams!

23rd Jan: I don't like the look of it. Is the weather breaking up? If so God help us, with the tremendous summit journey and scant food.

18th Feb: Pray God we get better travelling as we are not so fit as we were and the season advances apace.

5th Mar: God help us, we can't keep up this pulling, that is certain. Among ourselves we are unendingly cheerful, but what each man feels in his heart I can only guess.

29th Mar: It seems a pity, but I do not think I can write more.

R. Scott

For God's sake look after our people.

> 🔑 **KEY POINT**
>
> Although the terms 'diary' and 'journal' are often used interchangeably, the expectations are different for exam purposes. A diary is often a purely personal and private record, written in a **colloquial** style or even in notes, and often consisting of very short entries. A journal is likely to be a formal record of a journey or significant experience, intended for a wider audience and possibly for publication. It is therefore written in full sentences and with some consideration of style.

7 With your partner, list the common characteristics of the style of writing used in journals (also remember the journal extracts in Activity **18** of Unit **1**). They are obviously written in the first person – using *I* or *we* – but what can you say about the following:

  a tense?

  b **register**?

  c vocabulary level?

  d sentence length?

  e sentence type?

  f content?

8 Imagine you are Captain Bob Bartlett in the passage in Activity 2. Write three journal entries, with dates, for the winter period of 1913–14, from the freezing of the sea to when you abandon ship.

Use the time grid from Activity 5 to help you. Do not simply retell the story – adapt the material. Write about 350 words, in an appropriate style, and refer to the following:

previous events and the original goal of the expedition

Stefansson's character and behaviour

the mood of the crew and their fears

how the crew passed the time

what happened to the *Karluk*

the journey you are about to face

your thoughts and feelings about the future.

9 The next passage concerns mountaineering. Discuss these questions with your partner:

a How do you feel about mountains?

b What makes some people determined to get to the top of them?

c What can go wrong during a climbing expedition?

d What do you think the title 'A rock and a hard place' means?

10 Read the article below, from a Sunday newspaper's magazine, which concerns the death of a mountain climber.

14

A rock and a hard place

Alison Hargreaves faced the toughest decision of her career. It was August 6: she had spent six weeks on K2 and had already failed in two summit bids. Now, should she stay and give it one more try? Or call it a day and go home?

The situation was as bleak as could be. Alison was back at base camp, its cluster of red and yellow tents pitched unevenly among the ice and boulders of the Godwin-Austen Glacier. Towering 12,000 ft above was K2 itself, shrouded in grey,

wind-tossed clouds. It was bitterly cold and raining and, says the American climber Richard Celsi, Alison was in tears.

By Celsi's account, Alison had changed her mind a dozen times. Now she was utterly torn. She wanted to fulfil her dream of climbing K2, adding it to Everest to become the only British woman to have reached the world's two highest summits. And she desperately wanted to be back with her children, Tom, six, and Kate, four.

The previous night she seemed to have made up her mind to leave. She had packed her equipment and said goodbye to the climbers who were staying. Her porters were due to leave at 7 a.m. and Alison had a flight booked from Islamabad in

a week's time. 'It was done,' says Celsi. 'She was going home.'

But early that morning, Alison reopened the question once again, drinking endless cups of coffee with Celsi as she turned it over and over in her mind. 'It was a very emotional thing for her,' says Celsi. 'She really went through a lot of things.' Finally, just 15 minutes before the porters were due to depart, she told Celsi she had decided to stay, reasoning that, since she had been away for so long, one more week wouldn't matter. 'She said it was logical to give the weather a chance to clear.'

Alison hugged Celsi and thanked him profusely for his help. In some haste, her equipment was retrieved. Celsi himself was leaving, and Alison gave him some letters and a fax saying she had decided to give K2 'one more try'. As he set off down the glacier, Celsi turned to look back at Alison, and saw her waving to him through the drifting rain. 'She seemed in good spirits,' he recalls. 'She had made her decision.'

Four days later Alison and a group of climbers left base camp for their summit bid. By August 12, they had reached Camp Four on a sloping snowfield known as the Shoulder, 2,000 ft below the summit. They set off before dawn the next morning, climbing a steep gully called the Bottleneck, passing beneath an unstable wall of ice pinnacles and finally emerging on the summit ridge.

At 6.30 p.m. the climbers in base camp received a radio call from the summit. Alison and three others had reached the top, and another two were about to arrive. The caller, a Spanish climber, added that there was no wind but it was bitterly cold, and they were about to start their descent. There was no further word.

An hour later the upper reaches of K2 were hit by hurricane-force winds. As they edged their way back down the summit ridge, Alison and her companions stood no chance. She was plucked from the ridge by the wind and hurled down K2's monumental South Face.

The next morning two Spanish climbers, Pepe Garces and Lorenzo Ortas, who had survived the storm at Camp Four, were descending the mountain suffering from frostbite and exhaustion. Some 3,000 ft below the summit they found a bloodstained anorak lying in the snow. They also saw three slide-marks leading towards the edge of an ice cliff. But above the cliff, some 600 ft away, they saw a body resting in a hollow. 'I recognised the red clothing,' Ortas says. 'I knew it was Alison.'

At 33, after a mercurial climbing career, Alison had become an icon – a symbol of what women could achieve. For some her death represented a betrayal of motherhood, for others a paradigm of the dilemmas faced by mothers seeking a career.

Alison had been bemused by the publicity her Everest climb attracted, saying: 'The whole thing is much bigger than I can handle.' But she was worthy of her acclaim. Her Everest ascent in May – alone and without using supplementary oxygen or porters – was a supreme moment of the sport. Just 5 ft 4 in and with an easy smile, she impressed people with her friendliness, modesty and charm. Some, accustomed to the ruthless egos of some leading male mountaineers, were relieved to find her so *normal*.

Yet Alison was far more complex than her image revealed. The climber who exulted in her triumph on Everest could be racked with doubt. She could be talkative and outgoing – or reticent and closed. She was eager to show that she was self-sufficient, yet ardent for approval and acclaim.

The most profound contradiction lay in her replies when asked the perennial question of why she climbed. She said she did so because she had something to prove – then added that, after each summit, she felt she had to prove herself again. So what was Alison trying to prove, and why was she never satisfied? And is it true that her ceaseless quest led inevitably to a reckless death?

Adapted from an article by Peter and Leni Gillman, *The Sunday Times*, 3rd December 1995.

11 With a partner, make a list of the similarities and differences between the experiences of those on board the *Karluk* and those of the K2 climbers.

12 With your partner, work on the following tasks:

   a Think of and list adjectives of your own which you could use to describe the character of Alison Hargreaves.

   b Agree on and list the characteristics of the style commonly used for informal letters to relatives.

13 Write Alison Hargreaves' last letter to her parents after deciding to stay. Use an appropriate style, and write about 300 words. Begin *Dear Mum and Dad*. Mention the following:

   ■ her difficult decision and how she made it

   ■ conditions on K2

   ■ her ambitions and expectations

   ■ her feelings about climbing

   ■ her feeling about her fellow climbers

   ■ her feelings about her family.

14 Read the leaflet below, which gives information about a youth outdoor-pursuits programme called 'The International Award'.

The International Award

What is it?
The Award is an exciting self-development programme for all young people worldwide. It equips them with life skills, builds their confidence and engages them with their communities. It gives all young people aged between 14 and 24, regardless of their background, abilities or circumstances, an opportunity to experience challenge and adventure, to acquire new skills and to make new friends.

What does the programme consist of?
It is a four-section programme, with three progressive levels: Bronze, Silver and Gold. Participants are in charge of their own programme, setting their own goals amd measuring their progress against them.

The Sections
• Service develops a sense of community and social responsibility
• the Adventurous journey cultivates a spirit of adventure and and an understanding of the environment
• the Skills section develops cultural, vocational and practical skills
• Physical Recreation encourages improved performance and fitness.

The Residential Project, an additional requirement at Gold level, broadens horizons through a worthwhile residential experience.

What are the benefits of involvement?
The Award is widely recognised by educationalists and employers. Some of the benefits to young people include developing or discovering:

• a sense of achievement
• new skills and interests
• self-confidence and self-reliance
• leadership skills and abilities
• exciting opportunities
• friendship
• experience of teamwork and decision making
• a network of local, national and international connections
• enjoyment.

Adapted from Fact Sheet, The Duke of Edinburgh's International Award, www.intaward.org

THE DUKE OF EDINBURGH'S INTERNATIONAL AWARD

15 Select the relevant material in the text, then use it to write the script for a talk to a group of fellow students in which you describe the Award programme and encourage them to take part. Write about 300 words.

  ■ Summarise the rules and structure of the programme.

  ■ Explain the aims and what is involved.

  ■ Comment on the benefits of taking part and give examples of your own.

16 Give your talk to the class, and be prepared to answer any questions your audience asks about the programme.

17 Read the internet advertisement below for courses in white water rafting.

WHITE WATER ACTION IN VICTORIA FALLS
The most exciting experience you'll ever have!

HOME   **OUR ACTIVITIES**   TRANSFERS   RESTAURANTS   PRICE LIST   DISCOUNT SPECIALS   CONTACT US

In 1985, Shearwater was the first Zimbabwean company to run commercial white water rafting trips in Victoria Falls, Zimbabwe. Since those first intrepid paddle strokes on the Zambezi River, Shearwater has become synonymous internationally with some of the best white water action on the planet in dramatic scenery otherwise hidden from visitors. Today, 28 successful seasons later, Shearwater continues to be at the forefront of white water rafting on the Zambezi, offering one-day rafting trips (in both high- and low-water seasons), overnight trips, and multi-day wilderness adventures. There's something to suit everyone. Dare you try it?

SPLASH AND DASH – approx. March and June

'Splash and Dash' describes a very high-water run operated at the beginning and end of the rafting season. Most of the really big, dramatic rapids, for which the Zambezi is famous, have either been washed out or are considered too dangerous for commercial rafting purposes. This stretch of the river from rapid 15 to rapid 24 is fast flowing but the rapids are quite gentle compared to other times of the year.

Considered more of a scenic trip, as the gorge and the river are breathtakingly beautiful following the rainy season, the whirlpools and boils can pose a few unexpected surprises for the unwary! The hike out of the gorge remains – as always – arduous, so you need to be fit!

US$132

MULTI-DAY RAFTING ADVENTURES – low Water Only

Shearwater's Multi-Day Rafting Adventures (2½ days or 5 days). A chance for you to explore more of the Zambezi River down to the Lower Muwemba Falls, past the Batoka Dam and on to where the land flattens out towards the upper reaches of Lake Kariba. The days get lazier as the river widens through flat terrain, and there is plenty of opportunity for you to fish, watch the wildlife and camp in the wilderness on the pristine sandy beaches of the Zambezi. Tents are provided, although you may choose to sleep directly under the glittering velvet canopy of an African night.

Shearwater offers 2½ day (US$550) and 5day (US$880) Multi-Day Rafting Trips.

OVERNIGHT TRIPS – low Water Only

Instead of facing an arduous climb at the end of an amazing day, take us up on our offer to camp overnight in the gorge on one of the pristine beaches used exclusively by Shearwater clients, and witness complete peace and privacy beside the river when everyone else has left. Accommodation is in tents although many people choose to sleep under the clear sky. Sit out under the African stars and relive the memories of your day's rafting around a campfire. Walk along the Batoka Gorge and transfer back to town after breakfast the next morning.

US$220 – Minimum of 4 required.

A certificate is awarded at the end of every trip in confirmation of conquering the mighty Zambezi River.

Adapted from www.shearwatervictoriafalls.com/rafting/

TASK TIP

Advertisements aim to persuade, using a mixture of the following devices:

- **imperative verbs**
- questions
- exclamations
- **clichés**
- short/non-sentences
- repetition
- superlatives and **intensifiers**
- personal pronouns *you*, *we* and *our*
- evocative / emotive adjectives
- **alliterative** phrases
- rhyme
- statistics.

These stylistic features make the text as easy as possible to read, understand and remember, and they entice and pressurise the reader into accepting the offered product by making it sound a desirable thing to own or to do. The content is entirely positive, and usually begins with an attention-catching device, followed by evidence and details to support the initial claim. These devices can be used in all types of persuasive writing.

18 What are the stylistic features of written advertisements? Give examples of each from the passage above, and explain how they aim to persuade.

19 Write an informal letter or email of about 250 words to a friend to suggest that you both go on one of the trips. (Pretend it is in your own country.)
   - Give a summary of the factual information.
   - Give your impression of the company.
   - Give reasons why it would be a good idea to go on such a trip.
   - Say which of the trips sounds most attractive and why.

20 Formal letters, whose aim is usually to persuade or argue, have the following format, which you would use when writing for official or business purposes, or to someone whom you have never met.

Dear Madam/Sir (or the official position)

or

Dear Mr/Ms (Surname) (if you know his/her name)

Section 1: Reason for writing / topic of letter

Section 2: Background to and details of request / complaint / issue

Section 3: Conclusion, threat, thanks, prediction, advice, warning

Yours faithfully (if you have not addressed the recipient by name)

or

Yours sincerely (if you have addressed the recipient by name)

Example of letter text:

I am writing to you because of an incident I witnessed recently in one of your stores, which made me feel angry and embarrassed.

Last Saturday afternoon I was with my family in your Barcelona branch, shopping for toys. An elderly man, who was alone, collapsed on the floor, and a nearby customer asked for an ambulance to be called. The member of staff at the pay counter said he was too busy, suggesting that the customer should use her mobile phone instead. Although the store was very busy that day, I do not believe this was an acceptable response from the member of staff, and my children and some foreign tourists were shocked by the lack of concern it revealed.

Unless such behaviour is your company policy, it seems that there is a need for your employees to be better trained in customer service, as this kind of incident damages your reputation with the public.

KEY POINT

Informal letters or emails tend to use contractions (e.g. *can't, OK*), **abbreviations** (e.g. *uni, probs*), **phonetic** spelling (e.g. *hilites, kwik*) and colloquial expressions (e.g. *no way, bonkers*) as if the writer is speaking aloud to the recipient, with whom he or she has a relationship. For assessment purposes, however, it is not appropriate for your response to be so casual, and at least some degree of formality is required for a written response to a text in reading or writing papers or coursework. Even if you are asked to write a letter to a relative, it is better to avoid slang, jargon or non-sentences, and to write in paragraphs, as the aim is to demonstrate that you can use accurate and mature written English.

21 Plan and write a letter of about 350 words to the editor of a local newspaper, giving your views on extreme sports after a recent reported incident in your area. You may argue *either* that extreme sports should be allowed *or* that they should be banned.

Use the ideas you collected in Activity **1**. Refer to the recent incident in your opening paragraph.

➕ Further practice

a Imagine that you and your friend went on a Shearwater rafting course and were not satisfied with the experience. Write a letter of complaint to the company and ask for your money back. Include references to the advertisement in Activity **17**.

b Imagine that you are on an International Award expedition which has met with unforeseen difficulties. Write a journal entry describing your situation, location, fellow expeditioners, thoughts, feelings, and giving a prediction of what will happen next.

c Describe a sport you are keen on – either as a spectator or as a participant – in a letter to an acquaintance who is not familiar with it but whom you want to persuade to become involved in it.

19

KEY POINT

Formal letters differ from informal letters in register and in having a clear and conventional structure: usually one paragraph per section, although the middle section can extend over two or three paragraphs. The tone of a formal letter is impersonal and polite – even when complaining – and the expression is formal (i.e. in complex sentences and without contractions, abbreviations or colloquialisms). It is not usually necessary to date or give addresses in an exam letter, though these would be essential for a real letter.

KEY POINT

In writing papers you may be given a choice of composition titles belonging to the two genres of descriptive and narrative, and you may have the option to write a descriptive piece for a coursework portfolio. Although narratives need to contain some description of character and setting, the two kinds of writing are fundamentally different, so it is important not to confuse them. You may be better at one kind of writing than the other, and this will help you choose. Although the process and the kind of titles set are not usually the same for exams and coursework, the skills needed to produce appropriate, engaging and high-quality continuous writing are the same.

20

Unit 3: Continuous Writing

This unit introduces descriptive writing for compositions and coursework assignments. It focuses on the skills of using adjectives and imagery to convey a scene or character, and explains ways of structuring descriptive writing.

1   Write definitions of **narrative** and **description**, then offer them to the class for discussion of the differences between the two **genres** of writing.

2   Are the following statements about descriptive writing true or false?

   a   Descriptive writing must be based on the truth.

   b   You need a wide vocabulary to be good at descriptions.

   c   It is difficult to make descriptive writing interesting.

   d   Descriptive writing is the easier choice.

   e   You should use only the sense of sight when describing something.

   f   Descriptive writing doesn't have a structure.

   g   You don't need to write in full sentences for description.

   h   Descriptions are often written in the present tense.

   Discuss your views in class.

3   Write words (including colours) that come to mind when you consider the following **moods** or atmospheres.

   - loneliness
   - decay
   - celebration
   - tranquillity
   - fear
   - love.

KEY POINT

Descriptive compositions may be real or imagined, but try to base your description on an actual memory or experience. This will make your response more convincing and original, and it will be easier for you to think of material. Use of the present tense gives a sense of immediacy. Your ability to structure varied and sophisticated sentences is assessed and you should avoid using non-sentences. Don't start every sentence with *There is* or *The storm* or *It*, however, but vary the subject and verb in each sentence. Try to include a range of the following:

- unusual vocabulary
- varied vocabulary
- as many of the five senses as possible
- multiple adjectives
- **similes** and **metaphors**
- varied sentence lengths
- sound effects (e.g. **alliteration**, **onomatopoeia**).

TASK TIP

Adjectives are the key to effective descriptive writing; nouns need to be qualified by at least one adjective, and usually more, to enable the reader to picture what is being described, whether a person, place or object. The more precise, varied and uncommon your use of adjectives, the more the reader will be able to picture and engage with your description. Atmosphere can best be created by appealing to all five senses: sight, sound, smell, touch, taste. Colour is essential for conveying mood, and size and shape are also important elements in descriptive writing. When more than one adjective is used before a noun, size and shape adjectives go first, colour next, and other types of adjective closest to the noun (e.g. *the large, silver-framed, speckled, antique mirror; the tiny, square, black, velvet-covered box*).

TASK TIP

The man was walking along the street is much less effective than *The ancient bearded tramp in his tattered grey overcoat and filthy shoes was shuffling along the damp and littered pavement*. Verbs of locomotion describe more than just movement: they can convey the gender, age, social status, health, mood and personality of the character.

4 For each of the following scenes, write a descriptive paragraph, covering as many senses as possible. Think about your own experience of such events.

   a a street market in summer in a hot climate

   b an outdoor festival in winter in a cold climate

Read some of your paragraphs to the class for comparison and comments.

5 Look at the underlined words in the following sentences and replace them with more unusual and ambitious adjectives.

   a The students had a <u>good</u> day out.

   b The weather yesterday was <u>bad</u>.

   c I think your new dress is very <u>nice</u>.

   d The film I saw last night was <u>awful</u>.

   e What a <u>pretty</u> view!

6 Rewrite the following phrases, adding two adjectives before each noun. Think of adjectives with interesting sounds and avoid clichés (obvious and common phrases such as *busy street* or *delicious food*).

   a the house on the corner of the street

   b the girl with the cat in the garden

   c the car in the car park by the river

   d the meal in the restaurant in the city centre

   e the students in the school in the suburb

Now extend each of your rewritten phrases into full sentences using verbs and adverbs which are unusual, precise and vivid.

7 With your partner, list all the verbs you know which refer to a manner of walking (e.g. *shuffle*). Now use a thesaurus to add to your list. See which pair in the class can get the longest list in ten minutes. (Make sure that you understand what the words mean.) Write the words which are new to you in your personal vocabulary list, with an example of usage.

8 Read the novel extract below about the sinking in the Pacific of a cargo ship on which an Indian boy called Pi is travelling to Canada with his family and the contents of Pondicherry Zoo.

It was dark still, but there was enough light to see by. Light on pandemonium it was. Nature can put on a *thrilling show*. The stage is vast, the lighting is dramatic, the extras are innumerable, and the budget for special effects is absolutely unlimited. What I had before me was a spectacle of wind and water, *an earthquake of the senses*, that even Hollywood couldn't **orchestrate**. But the earthquake stopped at the ground beneath my feet. The ground beneath my feet was solid. I was a spectator safely ensconced in his seat.

It was when I looked up at a lifeboat on the bridge castle that I started to worry. The lifeboat wasn't hanging straight down. It was leaning in from its davits. I turned and looked at my hands. My knuckles were white. The thing was, I wasn't holding on so tightly because of the weather, but because otherwise I would fall in towards the ship. The ship was listing to port, to the other side. It wasn't a severe list, but enough to surprise me. When I looked overboard the drop wasn't sheer any more. I could see the ship's great black side.

A shiver of cold went through me. I decided it was a storm after all. Time to return to safety. I let go, **hotfooted** it to the wall, moved over and pulled open the door.

Inside the ship, there were noises. Deep structural groans. I stumbled and fell.

No harm done. I got up. With the help of the handrails I went down the stairwell four steps at a time. I had gone down just one level when I saw water. Lots of water. It was blocking my way. It was surging from below *like a riotous crowd*, raging, frothing and boiling. Stairs vanished into watery darkness. I couldn't believe my eyes. What was this water doing here? Where had it come from? I stood **nailed** to the spot, frightened and incredulous and ignorant of what I should do next. Down there was where my family was.

I ran up the stairs. I got to the main deck. The weather wasn't entertaining any more. I was very afraid. Now it was plain and obvious: the ship was listing badly. And it wasn't level the other way either. There was a noticeable incline going from bow to stern. I looked overboard. The water didn't look to be eighty feet away. The ship was sinking. My mind could hardly conceive it. It was *as unbelievable as the moon catching fire*.

Where were the officers and the crew? What were they doing? Towards the bow I saw some men running in the gloom. I thought I saw some animals too, but I dismissed the sight as illusion **crafted** by rain and shadow. We had the hatch covers over their bay pulled open when the weather was good, but at all times the animals were kept confined to their cages. These were dangerous wild animals we were transporting, not farm livestock. Above me, on the bridge, I thought I heard some men shouting.

The ship shook and there was that sound, *the monstrous metallic burp*. What was it? Was it the collective scream of humans and animals protesting their oncoming death? Was it the ship itself giving up the ghost? I fell over. I got to my feet. I looked overboard again. The sea was rising. The waves were getting closer. We were sinking fast.

I clearly heard monkeys shrieking. Something was shaking the deck. A gaur—an Indian wild ox—**exploded** out of the rain and **thundered** by me, terrified, out of control, berserk. I looked at it, dumbstruck and amazed. Who in God's name had let it out?

From *Life of Pi*, by Yann Martel.

9 In groups of three, discuss and make comments for class discussion on:

   a the underlined phrases

   b the italicised phrases

   c the words in bold

   d how the description changes during the course of the passage

   e how an atmosphere of fear is created.

10 In the same style (short sentences and questions for dramatic effect) and using a range of powerful adjectives and verbs, write approximately another 150 words to continue the description of the sinking of the ship and the 'pandemonium' on board. Read it to the class.

11 A haiku is a kind of descriptive poem. Here are two examples:

Striking yellow bird	*Gold and scarlet leaves*
At a desert waterhole	*Rustle in the lively breeze,*
Dips its beak and drinks	*Skirting the mountain*

Haikus have five syllables in the first and third lines, and seven syllables in the middle line. They aim to describe a beautiful or impressive natural moment.

Write haikus for the pictures below. Draft and edit in order to arrive at the best possible versions to read out to the class. Remember to use specific vocabulary, and think about visual and sound effects.

23

12 Read the passage below from an **autobiography** set on the Greek island of Corfu.

The Strawberry Pink Villa

The villa was small and square, standing in its tiny garden with an air of pink-faced determination. Its shutters had been faded by the sun to a delicate creamy-green, cracked and bubbled in places. The garden, surrounded by tall fuchsia hedges, had the flower-beds worked in complicated geometrical patterns, marked with smooth white stones. The white cobbled paths, scarcely as wide as a rake's head, wound laboriously round beds hardly larger than a big straw hat, beds in the shape of stars, half-moons, triangles, and circles, all overgrown with a shaggy tangle of flowers run wild. Roses dropped petals that seemed as big and smooth as saucers, flame-red, moon-white, glossy, and unwrinkled; marigolds like broods of shaggy suns stood watching their parent's progress through the sky. In the low growth the pansies pushed their velvety, innocent faces through the leaves, and the violets drooped sorrowfully under their heart-shaped leaves. The bougainvillaea that sprawled luxuriously over the tiny front balcony was hung, as though for a carnival, with its lantern-shaped magenta flowers. In the darkness of the fuchsia hedge a thousand ballerina-like blooms quivered expectantly. The warm air was thick with the scent of a hundred dying flowers, and full of the gentle, soothing whisper and murmur of insects. As soon as we saw it, we wanted to live there – it was as though the villa had been standing there waiting for our arrival. We felt we had come home.

From *My Family and Other Animals*, by Gerald Durrell.

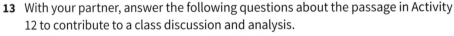

13 With your partner, answer the following questions about the passage in Activity 12 to contribute to a class discussion and analysis.

a What can you say about the adjectives used?

b Why do you think there are so many hyphenated (compound) adjectives?

c What sound effects are created?

d Can you find evidence of **personification** (describing things as if they were people)?

e How else has the author made the passage vivid?

TASK TIP

Imagery can contribute to powerful and memorable descriptive writing in the form of similes (stated comparisons using *as* or *like*, e.g. *as aloof as a cat*) and metaphors (implied comparisons, e.g. *the wind roared*). Imagery is meant to help the reader to picture something by comparing it to something else, so the comparison should be apt enough to be convincing but unusual enough to be interesting. Imagery can also include onomatopoeia to create sound effects, as in *The grandmother cooed over the baby*.

14 With your partner, discuss the following pairs of sentences. For each pair, say which sentence is more effective. Be prepared to explain your choice.

   a It was autumn and the trees were aflame.

   It was autumn and the leaves were reddish-brown.

   b The old man's face was wrinkled.

   The old man's face was like a withered apple.

   c Her laugh tinkled like ice in a glass.

   Her laugh was high-pitched.

   d The waiting passengers pushed onto the train.

   The waiting passengers stormed the train.

   e The rain drummed on the roof.

   The rain beat loudly on the roof.

15 It is likely that in Activity **14** you preferred the sentences which contain imagery. Here are more examples:

   a The hail stung the windows.

   b The sun stalked across the fields, as stealthily as a tiger.

   c The hillside bloomed with scarlet men marching.

   d Life's but a walking shadow.

   e The sea is like a giant, grey, hungry dog.

   f A lake is a river curled and asleep like a snake.

   Say whether each sentence above is a simile or a metaphor. Which image do you find the most effective as description. Why?

16 Copy and complete the following similes and metaphors using original but appropriate comparisons.

   a The baby's skin was as soft as . . . .

   b He leaped across the stream like . . . .

   c The train . . . its way through the mountain pass . . . .

   d She is as dangerous as a . . . .

   e The soldiers marched as if they . . . .

17 Rewrite the following sentences, using imagery to make the descriptions more detailed and specific.

   a The child was crying.

   b The house looked empty.

   c It started to rain.

   d The football stadium was crowded.

   e The woman got angry.

25

18 To test how effective a piece of descriptive writing is, try to draw what is being described. As you listen to the following extract from a science-fiction story being read to you, draw the creature.

> It came on great, oiled, resilient, striding legs. It towered twenty feet above trees, a huge evil god, folding its delicate watchmaker's claws to its oily, reptilian chest. Each lower leg was a piston, a thousand pounds of white bone sunk in thick ropes of muscle, sheathed over in a gleam of pebbled skin like the mail of a terrible warrior. Each thigh was a ton of meat, ivory and steel mesh. And from the great breathing cage of the upper body those two delicate arms dangled out in front, arms with hands which might pick up and examine men like toys, while the snake neck coiled. And the head, a ton of sculptured stone itself, lifted easily upon the sky. Its mouth gaped, exposing a fence of teeth like daggers. Its eyes rolled, ostrich eggs, empty of all expression save hunger.
>
> It ran, its pelvic bones crushing aside trees and bushes, its taloned feet clawing damp earth, leaving prints six inches deep wherever it settled its weight. It ran with a gliding ballet step, far too poised and balanced for its ten tons. It moved into a sunlit arena, warily, its beautiful reptile hands feeling the air.
>
> From *A Sound of Thunder*, by Ray Bradbury.

19 Is your picture complete and convincing? Compare it with your partner's and, if the pictures differ, try to justify yours by referring to descriptive details in the passage.

20 Describe a picture, photograph or postcard (given to you by your teacher or brought from home) of a countryside or town scene, while your partner – who must not be allowed to see your picture – draws what you are describing. Then swap roles and draw what your partner describes. Compare drawings with the original pictures: if the two pictures are very different, this may be either because you were not very clear or precise in your description, or because your partner did not respond accurately enough to the meaning of the words you used.

21 Imagine you are one of a class of students who lives on another planet and this is your first visit to Earth. Describe to the rest of your class a place you have visited and what happens there. You cannot mention the actual name of the place! For example, you might choose:

- a school ■ an athletics stadium ■ an airport
- a hospital ■ a theatre ■ a bowling alley

TASK TIP

Effective openings and endings always make a good impression in a composition. A strong descriptive opening will usually set the scene and refer to time, place, season or weather. A strong ending may draw a conclusion (e.g. *I shall never return to that place*), or refer back to the title (e.g. *And that was when I truly learned what homesickness was*), or to the beginning of the description (e.g. *After all, it was Friday the 13th*). It is better to write a description of a place at a specific time rather than a general one, which will be less focused on a particular atmosphere.

22 Look again at the first and last sentences of the passage in Activity **12**. Discuss with your partner whether or not they are effective, giving reasons.

23 With your partner, guess whether the following are openings or endings to pieces of descriptive writing.

  a It was the summer of 1996 and there had been a heatwave in Brasilia for over a week.

  b As far as I'm concerned, the future is not something to look forward to.

  c The impression will stay in my mind for the rest of my life.

  d The trip to Africa was all my grandmother's idea.

  e I hadn't really noticed the garden before the afternoon when my ball went over the wall.

24 Rank the following openings to descriptive compositions, according to how engaged you feel as a reader (1 = low; 5 = high). Write a comment for each one to explain your evaluation.

  a Imagine then a flat landscape, dark for the moment, but even so conveying to a girl running in the still deeper shadow cast by the wall an idea of immensity, of distance.

  b I think the best place I have ever visited is the football stadium in my town.

  c When I think of the year 2050, the first thing which comes into my head is a vision of bright lights.

  d The house my family moved to when I was six years old looked like a monster crouching on a hill waiting to pounce on and devour those foolish enough to pass by.

  e It was a fairy-tale turreted castle, which gave the impression that it had a sleeping princess in the attic and a heap of gold treasure in the dungeon, guarded by a fearsome, fiery dragon.

25 Write the first and last sentences for a composition on each of the following assignment titles:

  a Paradise Island

  b Home sweet home

  c The place that has most affected my life

  d Describe a place you visited which was not at all what you expected

  e Jungle

27

KEY POINT

Planning is an essential part of writing any composition, whether it is written for coursework or under timed conditions. It enables you to:

- give your writing structure
- build towards a climax or conclusion
- avoid repetition of material or vocabulary
- ensure focus and relevance
- achieve the required length
- provide sufficient supporting detail
- cover the title comprehensively
- concentrate on good expression and accuracy once you start writing.

If after a few minutes of thinking and planning you don't have at least six points to use in your composition, consider switching to a different title and starting again. Even when writing under timed conditions, you can afford to spend at least five minutes planning your composition. Plan in three steps:

1 Make a list, in a column, of topic headings (i.e. single words or short phrases), each of which could be developed into a paragraph.
2 Add supporting material in note form to each heading.
3 Order the headings logically, using numbers or arrows, according to the structure you have chosen.

26 Plan a descriptive composition on each of the two photographs below, entitled *Derelict house* and *Crowded market*. Make your structure and choice of opening and ending clear.

KEY POINT

Unlike a composition written under timed conditions, a coursework piece should be drafted as well as planned (and a draft of one of the coursework pieces may need to be included in your portfolio). It is essential to be aware that downloading and reproducing unaltered source material is viewed as **plagiarism**.

The purpose of the draft – which should be continuous writing – is to enable your teacher to comment on general aspects of its structure, length, content and accuracy, so that by following the advice given you can improve it in the next and final version. It is pointless to resubmit your draft as your final piece without revision (altering content) and editing (correcting expression). Your teacher is not permitted to point out or correct individual mistakes, so you need to proofread it carefully before you submit it for assessment.

27 Plan the following descriptive titles. What difference do the definite article and use of the plural make? List at least six ideas which could be developed into paragraphs, and make notes of some descriptive words, phrases and images you will include. Decide on the order in which you would use your material.

a The lake

b A place I never want to go back to

c Where I come from

d City street at night

e Mountains

29

KEY POINT

A particular event or time (e.g. sunset or a tropical storm) may help to give a focus and structure for a descriptive composition, but you must avoid responding in narrative mode to a descriptive title. Remember that the aim of description is to clearly convey a sense of place (or person) and atmosphere, not to give a series of events.

Structure can usually be provided by using a limited spatial or chronological framework, for example by movement to, through or around a building, or by recording how a scene changes during a short period of time. A movement towards a subject would allow you to go through the senses in the order that you experience them as you approach: *sight, sound, smell, touch* and *taste*. For example if you were walking towards the sea or towards a fruit market, this would be the order in which your senses would be evoked, ending with a sensation of saltiness or sweetness.

Avoid purely mechanical use of the senses, such as *there was a bad smell*. Be original and specific, for example *The odour of dead flowers reminded him of visits to the cemetery when he was a small child.*

➕ Further practice

a Write the composition for which you made the best plan in Activity **27**. Do not take more than one hour. Remember to check your writing when you have finished.

b Draw a sketch of the perfect house and label it. Use this sketch as the basis for a coursework draft with the title *My ideal home.* Your draft should be 550-800 words.

c As a coursework draft or for exam practice, write a descriptive composition entitled either *My nightmare landscape* or *My idea of heaven*. Plan and order the paragraph topics first, and check your writing afterwards.

KEY POINT

Content, structure, style and accuracy all feature in the assessment criteria for continuous writing. Leave enough time to check your work carefully in an exam. Checking is as important as planning, because it enables you to notice and correct careless errors, missing words or links, and unclear or clumsy expressions, which may otherwise reduce your mark. To achieve at a high level, your writing needs to be stylistically fluent and linguistically strong and accurate, including varied sentence structures, and without mechanical errors.

Read through your work as if you are the reader, not the writer, to ensure the following:

- It makes sense.
- It is cohesive and hangs together.
- It has no grammar, punctuation or spelling slips.
- The handwriting is legible.
- You have not repeated ideas.
- You have not over-used certain words.
- You have not used any awkward expressions.

Make late additions by putting an asterisk (*) within your writing and the extra sentence/paragraph at the end, or by putting a caret (^) to show that you are inserting an extra word or short phrase above the line. Cross out unwanted material with a neat, single horizontal line. (Correcting fluid is not allowed.) As long as your writing is legible, you do not need to worry about presentation. It actually gives a good impression that you have edited and tried to improve your work.

Part 2:
Work and education

Unit 4: Reading Comprehension

This unit focuses on extending vocabulary, selecting and organising material for summary, and responding to language to show explicit and implicit reading comprehension.

1 Read the newspaper article about Tom Hadfield to get the gist: Who? What? When? Where? Why? How?

2 You may not be familiar with some of the words in the article related to business.

   a Explain in your own words what a *whiz-kid* is, and why they are given this name.

   b Look at the context in the passage of each of the words shown on the left below, and match with its correct definition.

   c Add the words which you consider useful to your personal vocabulary list, with an example of usage.

evolved	ability to see commercial opportunities
potential	basic requirements, essentials
entrepreneurialism	unstable
volatile	purchasers of products
fundamentals	possibilities
innovative	developed gradually
consumers	administrative
executive	original

INTERNET GLOBAL LEADER

How an 18-year-old computer whiz-kid from the UK became an international 'Global Leader of Tomorrow'.

Soccernet.com

Tom Hadfield began using computers at the age of two and founded his first website when he was 12, developing it with his father into one of the most popular on the internet.

When asked how he managed to set up a website at such an early age, Tom says: 'It just <u>evolved</u> – it wasn't planned. When I was 12, I was putting football scores on the internet as a hobby and as it happened this turned out to have commercial <u>potential</u>.

'Both my dad and I had to learn as we went along since neither of us had any experience setting up businesses.'

Soccernet was sold for $40 million in 1999.

Hadfield was among 11 Britons under the age of 40 chosen as future global leaders by the World Economic Forum, an international non-profit-making foundation intended to promote <u>entrepreneurialism</u>.

Schoolsnet.com

The site at www.schoolsnet.com provides educational content for teachers, parents and students and acts as a resource for students who are applying for entrance to college.

The subjects of education and sport have been important to Tom at different stages in his life. 'As I have changed, my enthusiasm for football shifted to education. I was using the internet to revise for my A levels and I realised the pitfalls that exist in education websites. We have spent thousands of pounds on content for revision guides and we now offer the greatest supply of products for the education market.'

Is he worried that the mercurial internet bubble could eventually burst?

'Schoolsnet is confident that the <u>volatile</u> market conditions aren't going to affect us, as we possess good business <u>fundamentals</u>.' he said

AeroDesigns, Inc.

Tom Hadfield founded his latest site in 2009 after graduating from Harvard University, and now acts as its Chief <u>Executive</u> Officer.

The AeroDesigns family of products brings to <u>consumers</u> <u>innovative</u> systems that deliver powerful nutrient value and sensory pleasure in very small amounts. Tiny solid and liquid particles give light, convenient, personalised culinary enjoyment and healthcare by following the air into the mouth and landing on the tongue to give immediate taste and quick nutrition to the body.

33

3 Now read the article again, identifying the main facts about Tom Hadfield's career so far.

4 Copy the grid below and transfer the material you identified in the article into the appropriate boxes. As you transfer the main facts, change it into your own words and reduce it.

Tom Hadfield	
Soccernet	
Schoolsnet	
AeroDesigns	

5 With your partner, script a question-and-answer interview between Tom Hadfield and a young person who wants to set up a successful internet company. What questions could be asked in order to receive the answers in your boxes in Activity **4**? Write about 250 words. Begin with the interviewer asking: *How did you feel when you were named* 'a global leader of tomorrow'? Perform the interview for the class, taking one role each.

6 Read the following article about choosing where to go for higher education.

When you enter an Education Fair in your country, you'll be met by a huge array of displays with university representatives from English-speaking countries who will try to convince you that theirs is the right institution and in the right place for you.

It's best to have some idea of what you want to find out before you attend the Fair, or you'll emerge feeling bewildered and clutching a heavy pile of prospectuses, some of which you may not even read.

So do your homework: arrive with a checklist of questions.

What do I want to study?

This is a question only you can answer, of course. If you have no idea at all of what might be suitable for you, a visit to the Fair could well make up your mind. But it is, of course, better to arrive with some idea of what you'd like to do.

Most universities offer a wide variety of courses, from languages to business studies, literature to engineering. But if your aim is to go for the professions, such as medicine or dentistry, then your choice will be more limited.

Look at the prospectuses and try to get some idea of the universities which offer particular degrees. It is always best to have a choice.

- Does the university have a good record in dealing with overseas students?
- Does it have a special office to cater for the needs of international students?
- Does it have many international students there already and if so, from where?
- What support would there be, should things start to go wrong?
- Does it have a student counselling service?
- Is there an established student community from your country there already?

How much is it all going to cost?

Prices might vary considerably. Some degree programmes cost more than others – for example, laboratory-based courses such as medicine, veterinary medicine and dentistry will normally cost more than non-lab degrees.

But it's not just the course fees that you and your parents need to find on a yearly basis. There are many other things that will eat into your cash. You also have to budget for:

- accommodation and utility bills
- food
- books and equipment
- transport (how much will it cost to get from your lodgings to the campus?)
- clothing
- entertainment
- travel (how far is the university from an international airport?).

As a general rule, capital and large cities are more expensive than other parts of a country. But of course the bigger cities have more to offer in terms of cinemas, sports fixtures and cultural venues.

When thinking about cost, it is important to ask the representative of a prospective university how much you should expect to pay per year in living costs.

How will I know how good the degree is?

This is probably a better question to ask than 'Which is the best university?' The reason for this is that universities often specialise in particular fields, the newer ones tending to be strong in Art, Design and Media courses, while for subjects like science and medicine the older universities are still unrivalled. So before you make your mind up, here are a few more questions to ask:

- How many of the graduates get jobs?
- Is any work experience built in to the degree?
- How well qualified are the staff? Have they published any research? Do they actually do any teaching?
- How much teaching contact time will you get: how many lectures, seminars and tutorials per month?
- What do employers think of the degree, and what do current students think of it?
- Where does the university come in the national league tables for your subject?

Surprising though it may seem, many people make up their minds on the basis of people they know personally who have studied at a particular university, so if you know someone who's already taking a course that you think you might enjoy, it's well worth getting in touch with them. The sort of information they can give you will not be found in the university's prospectus.

What else is there to think about?

Taking a degree is primarily about education but it shouldn't be all work and no play. What happens outside your study and the lecture theatre is also important. For example:

- Do visiting bands or orchestras perform concerts regularly?
- Does the town organise an annual arts or science festival?
- Is the town on the rail network, so it's easy to get to other places?
- Is the town good for shopping?
- Is it an attractive place to walk around?
- Are the local people friendly?

Basically, there's so much to think about that you may end up being slightly confused, possibly even suffering from an acute case of information overload. But the important thing is to take your time: don't jump at the first offer that comes your way, for others are sure to follow.

KEY POINT

It is important to order facts and ideas in non-fiction writing, in summaries, arguments, discussions, evaluations, or for informative writing for coursework assignments. It is difficult for readers to take in the content or the purpose for which it is being used if the material is incoherent and has no logical progression.

7 a Skim the article and then give it a suitable title, of no more than six words.

b Scan the four sets of bullet points. For each set, write one or two sentences which include all the information/questions more briefly and concisely.

c Scan the unbulleted text. Identify the material which gives advice. Make two columns as shown below and fill them with short phrases, using your own words as far as possible. Examples have been provided to start you off.

Do	Don't
have some idea of what you are looking for	*collect too many prospectuses*

8 In small groups, read the jumbled sentences of the magazine article about working on a conservation project in Central China.

THE QINLING PANDAS

I had a wonderful childhood, living close to nature and having fun and adventures in the woods.

I was born close to the Qinling mountains, where our project is working to conserve giant pandas and their habitat.

Those memories and experiences are important to my own philosophy of life.

In the field, we visit project sites, doing interviews, giving presentations, conducting surveys, organising discussions, taking photos and gathering news.

Qinling is called the biological gene bank of China, with a large number of rare plants and animals, including the giant panda, crested ibis, takin, snub-nosed golden monkey, and many more.

I believe man has to respect nature, to live in harmony with it.

So by saving the forests for pandas, we also save other plants and animals.

Now I'm lucky enough to work for WWF to help giant panda conservation in Qinling.

In the office, I spend my time organising communication and awareness events and activities, collecting and editing news information, and preparing press statements and magazine articles.

A trip to a remote field site can last three or more days, depending on the distance and conditions.

The giant panda is not only the well-known icon of WWF and international conservation, it's also an umbrella species.

Although the Chinese government and the public are aware of the need for conservation, there's still much more to be done.

The panda is a very special animal and it's an honour for me to work for it, and to see the difference that the **support** from panda adopters is making.

Liang Hao, WWF China, *WWF Magazine* October 2013.

9 Use a copy of the text to re-sequence the material logically.

a Put the sentences in a cohesive order using numbers.

b Group them in paragraphs using arrows.

Be prepared to explain the reasons for your decisions.

10   Read the poem below about the daily work of an African woman.

Why the old woman limps

Do you know why the old woman sings?
She is sixty years old with six grandchildren to look after
While her sons and their wives are gone south to dig gold.
Each day she milks the goat, sells the milk to buy soap,
Feeds and washes the children, and tethers the goat.
In the evening she tells all stories of old at the fireside:
I know why the old woman sings.

Do you know when the old woman sleeps?
She rests with the dark, at night she thinks of
Tomorrow: she's to feed the children and graze the goat.
She's to weed the garden, water the seedling beans,
The thatch has to be mended, the barnyard cleared.
Maize pounded, chaff winnowed, millet ground, fire lit …
I do not know when the old woman sleeps.

Do you know why the old woman limps?
She goes to fetch water in the morning
        and the well is five miles away,
Goes to fetch firewood with her axe
        and the forest is five miles the other way,
Goes to the fields to look for pumpkin leaves
        leaving the goat tethered to the well tree
And hurries home to the children to cook:
I know why the old woman limps.

By Lupenga Mphande.

KEY POINT

When you are required to select evocative language from specified paragraphs in a passage, you should refer separately to each choice you make, rather than making a general or vague comment about all of them treated as a group. Furthermore, if the choice is a phrase, you need to examine the individual words within it. If your choices are too long, you will not demonstrate an ability to select appropriately from a text or give the necessary focus to individual words. However, selecting only part of a phrase may mean you miss an opportunity to comment on its full effect. You should always consider why the writer chose those particular words, rather than others which could have conveyed a similar meaning.

11 Now read the poem again, looking at how language not only conveys information but also implies feelings and attitudes.

Work in small groups to prepare answers to the following questions to contribute to a class discussion.

a In one sentence, describe the old woman's working life.

b List the ways in which her life is difficult.

c What are your feelings towards the subject of the poem?

d Select the words or phrases which evoke these feelings, and say why they have this effect on the reader.

e Say what you think the attitude of the poet is towards the old woman, giving reasons to support your answer.

12 Read the magazine article about working on the *Africa Mercy*, a hospital ship anchored off the coast of Sierra Leone.

> **VOCABULARY**
>
> **quarantined:** enforced isolation to prevent the spread of disease, originally for 40 days.

The deck of the cruise ship creaks and blisters in the west African sun. From beneath a weather-beaten lifeboat tarpaulin, a group of giggling school children hot-foot around enormous steel rigging bolts, as if each one is a piece of burning coal, before plunging headlong into the pool. From the upper tier of the vessel their laughter floats out across Freetown's war-ravaged harbour.

Home for the unique band of youngsters **frolicking** in the sparkling pool is a passenger ferry that once **plied** the Baltic. Rising above the harbour's grime, the gleaming vessel, formerly known as the *Dronning Ingrid*, is today the only sign of modernity on the entire coastline of Sierra Leone.

A 160 mt-long floating hospital, weighing 16,500 tons and accommodating 450 crew and medical staff, the *Mercy* is equipped with six operating theatres, intensive-care unit, recovery beds for 78 patients, an ophthalmic unit and two CT scanners. Over the next 12 months her staff will perform 7,000 operations.

The ship depends entirely on 2,000 volunteers from more than 40 nations, including surgeons, nurses, mechanics and teachers, all of whom pay for the privilege of living and working on board. The **annals** of the Mercy Ship are filled with **poignant** stories of lives transformed by simple surgery, some of which would take a mere 10 minutes in a typical modern western hospital.

Thousands live in **squalid** shacks, spilling sewage into the sea through open channels. Even the docks, where hessian sacks of cassava and rice rot on *the sweltering* quayside, <u>are</u> <u>a testament</u> to a state **ravaged** by decades of war. When the ship arrived, 12 people were injured in the *stampede* for free treatment.

Chief medical officer is Dr Gary Parker, <u>a legend among</u> surgeons and <u>the</u> <u>inspirational hub</u> of the ship. He lives with his wife and two children in two small cabins, and she teaches Latin to the floating classroom's pupils. Despite working a 70- to 80-hour week, he has no house, no car, no life savings and no pension. Parker has seen local children **mutilated** by rebels, and others outcast because of such disfiguring but treatable conditions as cleft palates. He is a world expert on head and facial injuries caused in war. However, the biggest threat to life is a **virulent** strain of cerebral malaria, which is now <u>on</u> <u>the offensive</u>.

13 With a partner:

   a Give synonyms, in the same part of speech, for the **ten** words in bold in the passage.

   b Use the **five** italicised words in the passage in sentences that show their meaning.

   c Explain in your own words the **five** underlined idiomatic phrases in the passage.

14 Write a summary of about 150 words to describe:

   a the people who live on the *Africa Mercy* ship

   b what they are doing there

   c the difficulties they face.

15 Comment on the effect of the use in the passage of the following phrases and grammatical structures:

   a *creaks and blisters*

   b *plunging headlong*

   c *gleaming vessel*

   d *no house, no car, no life savings and no pension*

   e *'Can you imagine ... Can you imagine ... Can you imagine ...?'*

Parker says, 'Some people may not understand how I can bring my children up on a boat off the west coast of Africa, but they have a full life here and a wonderful education. There are 50 children on board and, sure, they <u>live in a bubble</u>, but they are with their parents and are all remarkable and balanced individuals.

The school is perhaps the most unusual in Africa. With 50 youngsters aged between one and 18, the key challenge is not encouraging them to learn but filling their free time, since they are all largely **quarantined** to the ship and quayside. The *claustrophobia* on the ship can be intense, and the hardest thing is forming relationships. Although they all bond as one big family, this makes goodbyes very tough when people leave.

It is from the region's coastal trading posts, such as Freetown, that the **afflicted** come in their thousands for the public medical screenings held by *Africa Mercy*.

'Can you imagine one bucket and one bar of soap on each ward of 40 patients for all the nurses and caretakers to wash their hands? Can you imagine how hard it is to keep the linen and beds clean? Can you imagine working in a hospital where water rarely comes out of the tap? That is why the ship is here,' I'm told by Sandra Lako, a *Mercy Ship's* doctor, who now lives in Sierra Leone. Her story is amazing, but not unusual. She was raised on board and attended the school. Later,

she **emulated** the surgeons she admired as a child by becoming a doctor. I am told that most youngsters brought up on the boat return.

'The hardest thing about being here is the look in people's eyes when you say you can't help them,' says Sandra. 'We can only take on the most severe cases, those that have not gone beyond help. That's the truth we face. We cannot save everyone. The need is simply too great.'

Dan McDougall, *Sunday Times*, 21st August 2011.

40

TASK TIP

When you explain a process to someone, in speech or in writing, it is important to be factually accurate, to use short, concise expressions, and to get the instructions in the right order. Do not confuse the reader/listener with unnecessary information. You can use imperative verbs, and time adverbials such as *Next*, *Once*, *Then*, *After*, to make the sequence clear.

16 Using the map of Buenos Aires below, role play with your partner giving a visitor to the town directions how to get by car from:

   a the Plaza de Mayo to the Teatro Colon
   b the Congress Building to the Plaza San Martin
   c the Obelisk to the Parque Colon
   d Cafe Tortoni to Montevideo St
   e the Shopping Hall to the port.

17 Choose one of the routes listed in Activity **16** and put it in writing as a set of directions.

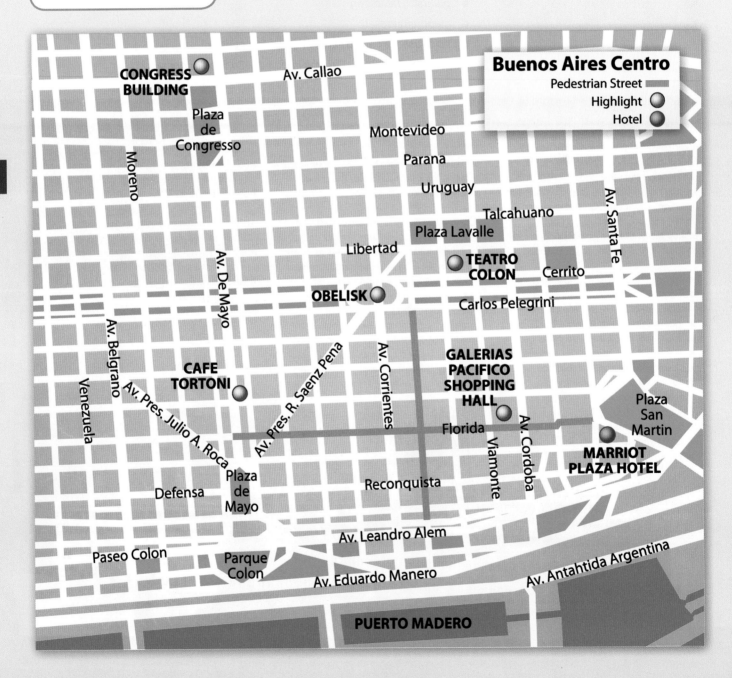

Further practice

a Write clear, concise and numbered instructions for how to tie a shoelace, put on a tie, plait hair or send a text message. Then ask someone to try to follow your instructions exactly!

b Think of a film you have seen recently. Write a one-paragraph summary of the **plot**, mentioning only the main aspects of the action, in chronological order, and grouping the information in complex sentences; for example *After a plane crash in a terrible storm, an American businessman finds himself alone on a desert island, which seems …*

c The chocolate cake recipe below has been jumbled up. Show the correct sequence by putting the instructions in order by number.

• Pour the mixture into the prepared tin and bake on the middle shelf of the oven for 30–35 minutes.

• Separate the yolks of five eggs from their whites and tip the yolks into a mixing bowl; put the whites into another bowl that is big enough to whisk them in.

• Place a heatproof bowl over a pan of simmering water. The water should be shallow and the bowl should be large enough to form a seal with the pan rim.

• Using a whisk, beat the yolks with 60 g of sugar and 60 g of self-raising flour until pale and creamy. Then beat the chocolate and butter mixture into the egg-yolk mixture. Beat the egg whites until they form soft peaks, then fold these into the chocolate mixture.

• Lightly grease the inside of a 20 cm tin with butter, then cut a strip of greaseproof paper that will wrap right around the inside of the tin. Next, cut a circle to fit the base.

• Test to see if it is cooked by sticking a skewer through the centre. Once cooked, leave to cool completely in the tin before serving.

• Break up the dark chocolate, place in the bowl and melt, then stir in thoroughly 60 g of butter and remove the bowl from the pan.

• Preheat the oven to 180°C or Gas Mark 4.

41

Unit 5: Response Writing

This unit focuses on news reporting and concentrates on the selection and transformation of information from a variety of fiction and non-fiction texts for text-based directed writing questions in reading papers and coursework assignments.

1   Read or listen to the passage from a novel set in the early 20th century about a young woman's first day at school as a teacher.

2   Work with a partner:

   a   Give synonyms for the **20** words in bold in the passage.

   b   Select **ten** words or phrases to show how the children felt about Ursula.

   c   Select **ten** words or phrases to show how Ursula felt about the children.

There was a **hubbub**, which gradually resolved itself into three columns of girls, two and two, standing **smirking** in the passage. In among the peg-racks, other teachers were putting the lower classes into **ranks**.

Ursula stood by her own Standard Five. They were jerking their shoulders, tossing their hair, nudging, **writhing**, staring, grinning, whispering and twisting.

A sharp whistle was heard, and Standard Six, the biggest girls, set off, led by Miss Harby. Ursula, with her Standard Five, followed after. She stood beside a smirking, grinning row of girls, waiting in a narrow passage. What she was herself she did not know.

Suddenly the sound of a piano was heard, and Standard Six set off **hollowly** down the big room. The boys had entered by another door. The piano played on, a march tune, Standard Five followed to the door of the big room. Mr. Harby was seen away beyond at his desk. Mr. Brunt guarded the other door of the room. Ursula's class pushed up. She stood near them. They glanced and smirked and shoved.

'Go on,' said Ursula.

They **tittered**.

'Go on,' said Ursula, for the piano continued.

The girls broke loosely into the room. Mr. Harby, who had seemed **immersed** in some occupation, away at his desk, lifted his head and thundered:

'Halt!'

There was a halt, the piano stopped. The boys who were just starting through the other door pushed back. The harsh, **subdued** voice of Mr. Brunt was heard, then the booming shout of Mr. Harby, from far down the room:

'Who told Standard Five girls to come in like that?'

Ursula **crimsoned**. Her girls were glancing up at her, smirking their accusation.

'I sent them in, Mr. Harby,' she said, in a clear, struggling voice. There was a moment of silence. Then Mr. Harby roared from the distance.

'Go back to your places, Standard Five girls.'

The girls glanced up at Ursula, accusing, rather **jeering**, fugitive. They pushed back. Ursula's heart hardened with **ignominious** pain.

'Forward—march,' came Mr. Brunt's voice, and the girls set off, keeping time with the ranks of boys.

Ursula faced her class, some fifty-five boys and girls, who stood filling the ranks of the desks. She felt utterly non-existent. She had no place nor being there. She faced the block of children.

Down the room she heard the rapid firing of questions. She stood before her class not knowing what to do. She waited painfully. Her block of children, fifty unknown faces, watched her, hostile, ready to jeer. She felt as if she were in torture over a fire of faces. And on every side she was naked to them. Of unutterable length and torture the seconds went by.

3   With a partner:

   a   Select **five** images from the passage (i.e. similes or metaphors).

   b   Explain the effect of the imagery you have chosen. Think about the **connotations** of the words, and what they make you think and feel.

   c   Find words that are repeated and explain the effect of the repetition.

4   Imagine you are the parent of a child in 'Standard Five'. Write a letter to the headteacher giving your views on why you think the new teacher should not have been appointed, using the ideas from the passage. Your letter should be about 300 words, in three paragraphs and include mention of:

   ■ her behaviour towards the pupils and the way she teaches

   ■ her attitude to her colleagues and her relationship with them

   ■ the way things are likely to develop in future.

   Begin your letter: *My daughter has told me about her new class teacher and I am writing to tell you that I am not satisfied ...* Before you start, read the Key point.

   Then she gathered courage. She heard Mr. Brunt asking questions in mental arithmetic. She stood near to her class, so that her voice need not be raised too much, and **faltering**, uncertain, she said:

   'Seven hats at twopence ha'penny each?'

   A grin went over the faces of the class, seeing her commence. She was red and suffering. Then some hands shot up like blades, and she asked for the answer.

   The day passed incredibly slowly. She never knew what to do, there came horrible gaps, when she was merely exposed to the children; and when, relying on some **pert** little girl for information, she had started a lesson, she did not know how to go on with it properly. The children were her masters. She **deferred** to them. She could always hear Mr. Brunt. Like a machine, always in the same hard, high, inhuman voice he went on with his teaching, **oblivious** of everything. And before this inhuman number of children she was always at bay. She could not get away from it. There it was, this class of fifty collective children, depending on her for command, for command it hated and resented. It made her feel she could not breathe: she must suffocate, it was so inhuman. They were so many, that they were not children. They were a **squadron**. She could not speak as she would to a child, because they were not individual children, they were a collective, inhuman thing.

   Dinner-time came, and stunned, **bewildered**, solitary, she went into the teachers' room for dinner. Never had she felt such a stranger to life before. It seemed to her she had just **disembarked** from some strange horrible state where everything was as in hell, a condition of hard, **malevolent** system. And she was not really free. The afternoon drew at her like some **bondage**.

   From *The Rainbow*, by D.H. Lawrence.

5 Read the following news report, noticing the order in which the information is given.

RESCUERS FIND TRAPPED STUDENT CAVERS ALIVE

Eight Swiss **potholers** trapped in a cave in eastern France by rising water were found alive yesterday. Rescue teams were preparing to work through the night to bring them to the surface.

Known as Bief-du-Paraud, the cave, which runs for 380 metres but only about 6 metres below the surface, is normally considered a beginner-level site for potholers.

The expedition had been part of a project for the students to develop their ability to face challenges.

Inexperienced, poorly equipped and with one of the group being partially blind, the students were initially given little chance of survival.

The potholers had entered the long narrow cave on Wednesday despite warnings from local people to stay away because rain in recent weeks had made the area dangerous.

Hope for the survival of the three women and five men – students and a teacher in their twenties – had been fading when they were found before midday by a diver who swam through a narrow passage to reach a chimney where they had taken refuge.

The diver discovered them crouched in the corridor above the water level 70 metres into the cave at Goumois in the Doubs département, 50 kilometres from the Swiss border. They had been trapped there for nearly 40 hours by sudden flooding on Wednesday.

Distraught relatives who had gathered at the site gave a cheer when news of their discovery was announced. The group was expected to be brought out through a hole being drilled into the chimney where they had taken refuge.

Rescuers were pumping water from the cave to avert flood danger from heavy rains over the past 24 hours. Two divers, one of whom is a doctor, were spending the night with the students in the chimney. They brought them food and water and a heating appliance.

'The group took refuge in a dry spot in a chimney,' Eric Zipper, technical adviser to the Upper Rhine cave rescue service, said. 'They are in good shape considering their ordeal. They are hungry and a little weak. They have very little food left, but they are in good spirits. There was no panic. They had a little light because they had rationed their batteries.'

Local potholing experts described the expedition as foolhardy, given the dangerous prevailing conditions. 'They were equipped only with walking shoes, jeans and anoraks,' M. Zipper said.

Markus Braendle, director of the Social Workers College of Zurich, where most of the students come from, said: 'I am so happy this nightmare is over.'

The French authorities are expected to start a legal inquiry into the conduct of the group's leader, a normal practice in such incidents.

Adapted from *The Times*,
19th May 2001.

44

❝ VOCABULARY

potholer: person who explores caves and underground holes

TASK TIP

Unlike other accounts of events, which are usually chronological, news reports generally follow this order:

1 summary of recent event
2 background to event
3 return to immediate situation
4 response of those involved
5 look ahead to near future.

The first few sentences answer the questions: *Who? What? When? Where?*, followed by *How?* and *Why?* Reporting does not include the emotional response or personal views of the reporter, or any direct address to the reader.

TASK TIP

Headlines are a summary in note form, leaving out unnecessary words. Their aim is to attract interest in the minimum amount of space and to sensationalise an event. Headlines tend to:

- consist of three to six words
- contain dramatic vocabulary (e.g. *crash*, *tragic*)
- use short words
- use the shortest synonym (e.g. *weds* for *marries*)
- use abbreviations, initials and acronyms (e.g. teen, Dr, EU)
- use the present tense for events in the recent past
- leave out definite and indefinite articles (i.e. *the* and *a*).

Future events may be indicated by the infinitive, as in *Minister to resign*. The passive is expressed by the past **participle** only, as in *Baby snatched by croc*.

6 With your partner, look again at the report and assign each paragraph a letter according to the following key:

a responses of participants or witnesses
b speculation about future developments
c facts about what happened
d expansion and background details of story
e official statements by the authorities involved
f description of what is happening now.

7 The headline of the next text about climber Alain Robert is typical of newspaper reports. Other examples are given below.

With a partner, discuss and list the common characteristics of headlines.

Dingo attacks child on beach

Riot halts match – 23 injured

Scandal Rocks Paradise Island

BLIND MOUNTAINEER CONQUERS EVEREST

Talented teen touts for trade

TIME RUNS OUT FOR WATCHMAKER

Markets plunge after shame shock

8   Headlines are sometimes difficult to understand because their grammar is so condensed. With your partner, answer these two questions for each of the following (real) headlines:

   a   What does it mean?

   b   How can you make the meaning clearer? Use more words if necessary, or change the word order or punctuation.

      i   *17 aliens held*

      ii   *500-year-old child found*

      iii *Squad helps dog bite victim*

      iv   *Miners refuse to work after death*

      v   *Wage rise bid defies ban*

9   Popular newspapers like to use the following devices in their headlines (see also the Spiderman headline):

   ■ puns – J*apanese yen for success*

   ■ **assonance** – *Hit list twist*

   ■ alliteration – *Fears of free fall*

   ■ quotations – *For richer, for poorer*

   ■ misquotations – *To buy or not to buy?*

   With your partner, find or make up examples of each kind of word play.

10 The paragraphs in the following report have been jumbled. With your partner, sequence them according to the usual structure of a news report by numbering the paragraphs 1 to 16.

11 With your partner, give synonyms for the **ten** words in bold in the report.

12 Give the report an alternative headline and a sub-heading.

TASK TIP

A sub-heading at the beginning or within a news report is a dramatic one-word or short-phrase summary – often a quotation – of the next section of the report. It signals a change of direction or prepares the reader for what will follow, and entices the reader to read on. It also breaks up the text to make it seem more accessible.

46

HOME NEWS GALLERY HELP CONTACT

SPIDERMAN CLIMBS SKY HIGH

Robert, who has gained fame – and **notoriety** – for scaling some of the world's tallest skyscrapers without permission, climbed the 191-metres-tall TotalFinaElf building in Paris before being **apprehended** by the city police.

Robert says he intends to continue his career of **conquering** the world's highest office blocks, using no climbing equipment except for a small bag of chalk and a pair of climbing shoes.

Daredevil French climber and urban sherpa Alain Robert added one of France's tallest office towers to his **tally** on Tuesday before scaling back down into the arms of the waiting police.

The crowd which gathered to watch the man, who is sometimes called the French Daddy-long-legs or the Human Spider, may have **unwittingly** tipped off police to what was going on.

Although Robert has **courted** arrest several times in the course of his urban climbing career, the French police are known to be a lot more sympathetic towards the local Spiderman than police in many other parts of the world.

'It was a little more difficult than I'd expected because of the wind, because of the sun,' Robert told Reuters after his **vertiginous** conquest. 'Sometimes it was a bit slippery,' he said, adding that the windows had just been washed.

Using his bare hands and **dispensing with** safety lines, Robert took about 90 minutes to reach the top of the headquarters of the oil corporation TotalFinaElf in the city's crowded La Défense business district.

Robert was apprehended on Tuesday, but not **charged**. According to local media reports, the police even offered him orange juice.

The law has not always been so good to Robert. In March, Chinese authorities refused him permission to climb the 88-storey Jinmau building in Shanghai, China's then-tallest building. He did so, once again wearing a Spider-Man costume , and was later arrested and jailed for five days, before being expelled from China.

In November last year, Singapore's police arrested Robert for attempting to scale the 280-metre Overseas Union Bank tower. And in April 1998, Parisian police arrested the stuntman after he climbed up the Egyptian obelisk in the Place de la Concorde and cheekily made a call on his cell phone from the top.

A mountaineer by training, Robert's first urban **feat** took place in his hometown of Valence, when the then-12-year-old scampered up to enter his family's eighth-floor apartment after losing his keys.

He was, however, given permission to climb the 200-metre high National Bank of Abu Dhabi, UAE, watched by about 100,000 spectators.

Now aged 50, his conquests have included the Sydney Opera House, the Sears Towers, the Empire State building, the Eiffel Tower and what was then the world's highest skyscraper, the Petronas Twin Towers in Kuala Lumpur, Malaysia, where he was arrested for criminal trespass on the 60th floor.

After climbing the New York Times Building in New York City on 5th June 2008, he unfurled a banner with a slogan about global warming that read 'Global warming kills more people than 9/11 every week.'

On 28th March 2011, Robert climbed the tallest building in the world, the 828-metre Burj Khalifa tower in Dubai, taking just over six hours to complete the climb.

However, he used a harness in accordance with safety procedure.

Adapted from www.abcnews.go.com

47

BANK ROBBER ESCAPES
JOHN STUART GLADWIN

Aliases: Michael Carmen, John Goodwin and Dennis H. McWilliams.

DESCRIPTION

Date of birth:	26th June, 1979	*Sex:*	Male
Place of birth:	Miami, Florida	*Hair:*	Black
Nationality:	American	*Eyes:*	Green
Height:	1.83 m.	*Complexion:*	Medium
Weight:	77 kilos	*Distinguishing marks:*	Scar on chin, earring in left ear
Build:	Medium	*Occupation:*	Construction worker

CAUTION

JOHN STUART GLADWIN, WHO IS BEING SOUGHT AS A PRISON ESCAPEE, WAS AT THE TIME OF HIS ESCAPE SERVING A LENGTHY SENTENCE FOR VIOLENT ROBBERY. HE IS BELIEVED TO BE ARMED WITH HANDGUNS AND A 9 MILLIMETRE RIFLE. HE IS CONSIDERED TO BE EXTREMELY DANGEROUS. IF YOU HAVE ANY INFORMATION CONCERNING THIS PERSON, PLEASE CONTACT YOUR LOCAL LAW-ENFORCEMENT OFFICIAL.

REWARD

A **$50,000** reward is being offered for information leading directly to the re-arrest of John Stuart Gladwin.

TASK TIP

News reports typically have the following stylistic features:

- short sentences – simple or **compound** (i.e. using *and*, *but*, *so*)
- short paragraphs – often consisting of only one sentence
- direct speech – to give realism and immediacy
- **reported speech** – introduced by a variety of verbs
- strings of adjectives – in front of nouns to describe them
- sensational vocabulary – to give a sense of drama.

After selecting relevant material in response to the questions on a reading paper, it is necessary to group and sequence it so that your response shows your understanding of the material. The logical order, or the order required by the response genre, is not always the order in which the text presents the material. It counts as mechanical use of the text if you do not modify the structure and language of the original.

13 Look at the 'wanted' poster. Work with your partner on the following tasks, both of you making notes. Use the material given, but also make inferences.

  a Select the information in the poster that you would use as a journalist writing a news report about Gladwin's escape.

  b Provide likely extra details about the fugitive, such as his family background, education and general state of mind.

  c Fill in the possible details of his escape: Where? From whom? When? How?

  d Imagine how he committed his original crime of robbery, and why.

  e Think of three different headlines for a report on the escape.

14 List all the alternatives to the verb *said* that can be used in news reports. Refer to the reports in Activities **5** and **10** for help.

15 Scan the following passage. Then write adjective 'strings', separated by commas, to fill in the **12** gaps. Hyphenated adjectives are allowed – and encouraged! (Journalists use them as a space-saving device.) For example, gap (e) could be filled by *home-made, comic, carnival-type*.

> Two (a) … robbers failed in their (b) … attempt to stage a (c) … robbery at a (d) … bank on Tuesday. Wearing (e) … masks and waving (f) … pistols, they threatened (g) … bank staff. Tellers handed over money, but one (h) … robber dropped the (i) … bag. Cursing, he tore off the mask when he could not see where it was, in full view of the (j) … camera. (k) … staff watched the (l) … police burst into the bank and escort the robbers away.

16 Turn the following set of reporter's notes, taken at a murder trial, into a news report for a national daily newspaper. Include a headline.

> Durban – 15th Feb 2012, 2 a.m. – woman living alone – Senne Wahl – ground floor block of flats – robbed and battered to death – only witness neighbour Lindi Madyo – 56-yr-old widow – heard disturbance – saw defendant throw hammer and gloves in bushes – described distinctive bulging eyes – defendant Jakob Peters claimed with wife at home all evening – defendant's identical twin brother Abel stood up in court – wearing same navy suit – same eyes – witness confused – couldn't confirm identity – defendant acquitted – lack of evidence – twins left court together laughing

17 Now you are ready to write a response to the poster in Activity 13. You work for a local newspaper and have been assigned to write the front-page story to be published the day after Gladwin's escape from custody took place. Using the notes you made in Activity **13**, report the information in an appropriate order and style. Give your report a headline and a sub-heading.

➕ Further practice

a You are tired of your school uniform! Use the following rules as the basis for a letter to the headteacher asking for changes. You may wish to comment on gender discrimination, outdatedness, cost, discomfort or inconsistency.

b Write a conversation between yourself and a friend: you agree with the idea of school uniform, but your friend does not. Set out your conversation in the form of a script of about 300 words. Use the school uniform rules provided to provide detail.

c Read the news article below. Use the information contained in the article to write a letter to encourage people to knit jumpers for Tasmanian penguins. Add extra information that can be inferred from the report and the picture. Begin your letter *Dear Penguin Lover …*

Rules for School Uniform

Boys, Years 7–11 (first year to fifth year): grey trousers, blue pullover, white long-sleeved shirt, school tie, grey socks, black leather shoes

Girls, Years 7–11: tartan skirt, red pullover, white long-sleeve blouse, school tie, white socks, brown leather shoes

Boys, Years 12 and 13 (sixth form): grey trousers, single-coloured shirt, school tie, formal jacket, grey socks, black leather shoes

Girls, Years 12 and 13: skirt, white blouse, school tie, white socks, brown leather shoes

Boys PE: navy shorts, white T-shirt

Girls PE: red short pleated skirt, white T-shirt

Girls may wear stud earrings but no other jewellery; boys may not wear any jewellery (except for watches for both girls and boys).

Boys' hair must be neither too long nor too short. Dyed hair is not allowed for girls or boys.

50

KNITTERS OF THE WORLD SAVE PENGUINS FROM EXTINCTION

The penguins which live on the island of Tasmania off the southern coast of Australia are much smaller and more vulnerable than their better-known Antarctic cousins. Already an endangered species, these 'fairy penguins', as they are known locally, came face to face with the probability of extinction in 2001. A huge illegal dumping of oil in the sea where the penguins hunt led to their feathers becoming clogged with life-threatening oil.

Volunteers from the Tasmanian Conservation Trust cleaned up stricken penguins but found that the birds were going straight back into the oil slick to fish in their familiar hunting grounds. One of the volunteers had the idea that a woollen coat would protect the birds, and an appeal was printed in Aged Pension News, a free newsletter circulated to elderly Australians. It was picked up and re-broadcast worldwide by the BBC, and the Trust was stunned to receive huge numbers of woollen jumpers knitted by well-wishers from far afield.

Jo Castle, a spokeswoman for the Conservation Trust, explained that the pattern was based on one used for penguins in colder climates. 'It was re-designed for the little penguins in the southern hemisphere,' she said. 'They have come from everywhere, even as far away as Japan. Someone in New York asked for a pattern, but we haven't received the jumper yet.'

There is strong scientific logic behind the Trust's approach. Wool is naturally water-repellent and when the fibres become wet, a chemical reaction creates heat which keeps the penguins warm. The birds do not seem to like their new coats very much, but as Castle explains, 'The penguins are not very happy about them, but they cover them from neck to ankle which stops them preening themselves and ingesting poisonous oil.'

The pattern specifies that the jumpers should be 40 cm long, but leaves the colour up to the knitters, mostly elderly women. Clearly the idea has appealed to their imagination, and every imaginable colour and design has been sent in, including football-team strips, patchwork designs and even 'penguin' suits.

For now, the future of the fairy penguins looks assured: the Trust has stockpiled some of the thousand jumpers it received for use in any future oil spillage.

Unit 6: Continuous Writing

This unit looks at the language and structure of both informative non-fiction accounts and imaginative descriptive writing, to develop the skills for writing assignments.

1   Think about a trip or visit you went on with your school, either educational or for pleasure, long or short. Answer the following questions in note form.

   a   Where did you go, and why?

   b   How long were you away?

   c   Who was in the group?

   d   How did you get there?

   e   What time of year was it? / What was the weather like?

2   Make notes, using time markers, about five events which occurred on your trip. For example: *Tues 6 a.m. – breakfast outdoors in freezing cold; teacher found cockroach in cornflakes; Sophie said she wanted to go home*

3   Write an account of your school trip as if for your school magazine, using the material you planned in Activities **1** and **2** and developing each note into a sentence. Use paragraphs to represent time jumps.

4   Choose one of the events in your timeline in Activity **2** to turn into a piece of description. Draft a page of writing in which you expand and explore the moment using figurative language to capture the setting, atmosphere, your thoughts and feelings, and the reactions of the people who were present.

5   Read this description from a memoir set in Australia.

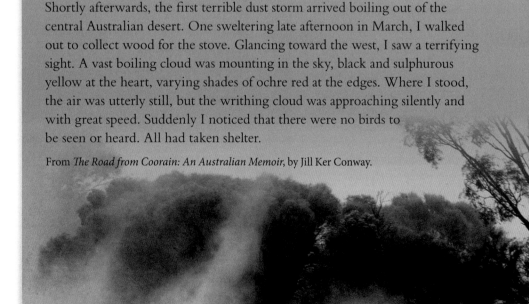

Shortly afterwards, the first terrible dust storm arrived boiling out of the central Australian desert. One sweltering late afternoon in March, I walked out to collect wood for the stove. Glancing toward the west, I saw a terrifying sight. A vast boiling cloud was mounting in the sky, black and sulphurous yellow at the heart, varying shades of ochre red at the edges. Where I stood, the air was utterly still, but the writhing cloud was approaching silently and with great speed. Suddenly I noticed that there were no birds to be seen or heard. All had taken shelter.

From *The Road from Coorain: An Australian Memoir,* by Jill Ker Conway.

TASK TIP

Factual material can be transformed into description by adding detail and changing the style in order to entertain and engage the reader rather than simply to inform them. Try to use original imagery to make your piece memorable. You are allowed to exaggerate the truth of appearance and behaviour to create an impression and/or to add humour. You should not stray into fantasy, however, as your description must be credible to enable the reader to imagine themselves present at the scene and share the experience or vision being described.

6 a Select the powerful words and phrases from the passage. Explain in a sentence for each why they are effective.

   b What is the overall impression given of the storm? Explain in one sentence the combined effect of the description.

   c Comment on how sentence structure contributes to effect.

7 Read this paragraph from a Victorian novel, describing an industrial town in northern England.

> It was a town of red brick, or of brick that would have been red if the smoke and ashes had allowed it; but, as matters stood, it was a town of unnatural red and black like the painted face of a savage. It was a town of machinery and tall chimneys, out of which interminable serpents of smoke trailed themselves for ever and ever, and never got uncoiled. It had a black canal in it, and a river that ran purple with ill-smelling dye, and vast piles of building full of windows where there was a rattling and a trembling all day long, and where the piston of the steam-engine worked monotonously up and down, like the head of an elephant in a state of melancholy madness. It contained several large streets all very like one another, and many small streets still more like one another, inhabited by people equally like one another, who all went in and out at the same hours, with the same sound upon the same pavements, to do the same work, and to whom every day was the same as yesterday and tomorrow, and every year the counterpart of the last and next.
>
> From *Hard Times*, by Charles Dickens.

8 Discuss in class:

   a the impression this description gives of the town

   b the words and phrases which convey this impression

   c the imagery in the passage.

   d the use of senses in the passage.

   e the words and grammatical structures which are repeated, and the effect of this repetition.

9 Read this paragraph from a novel describing the Marabar (Barabar) caves in India.

TASK TIP

You are likely to choose words or phrases which are images, or unusual, dramatic or atmospheric words which have connotations beyond ordinary meaning, as these are the ones which make an impression on the reader and evoke a response. Individual choices usually support each other and reinforce the writer's intended overall effect, for example danger or speed. Sometimes a key word is deliberately repeated; here it is *boiling*, which denotes both heat and movement. The length of sentences, especially when there is a sudden change, is a grammatical way of creating suspense or tension.

> The caves are readily described. A tunnel eight feet long, five feet high, three feet wide leads to a circular chamber about twenty feet in diameter. This arrangement occurs again and again throughout the group of hills, and this is all, this is a Marabar cave. Having seen one such case, having seen two, having seen three, four, fourteen, twenty-four, the visitor returns to Chandrapore uncertain whether he has had an interesting experience or a dull one or any experience at all. He finds it difficult to discuss the caves, or to keep them apart in his mind, for the pattern never varies, and no carving, not even a bee's nest or a bat, distinguishes one from another. Nothing, nothing attaches to them, and their reputation – for they have one – does not depend upon human speech. It is as if the surrounding plain or the passing birds have taken upon themselves to exclaim 'Extraordinary!' and the word has taken root in the air, and been inhaled by mankind.
>
> From *A Passage to India*, by E.M. Forster.

10 Discuss with a partner:

    a how the description has been structured, i.e. how it changes from beginning to end

    b the role played by grammatical choices in the description

    c how you would summarise in one sentence of your own words what you have learned about the place from this piece of description.

11 Plan and then write a description (about 200 words) of an extreme event or place, using as a model one of the three passages in Activities **5**, **7** or **9**. Think about both vocabulary and grammar, and about how the feelings of the observer are conveyed without them needing to be explicitly stated (e.g. fear, disapproval, awe). Read your description to the class for them to guess which passage you have based it on.

12 Read the informative account below, which is a web article describing a typical wedding ceremony in the Pennsylvanian Amish community. The Amish are a Protestant religious group which aims to preserve the simple and non-technological lifestyle of the early 18th century.

What's an Amish wedding like?

A typical Amish wedding day begins at 4 o'clock in the morning. After all, the cows must still be milked and all the other daily farm chores need to be done. There are also many last-minute preparations to take care of before the wedding guests arrive. Helpers begin to arrive by 6.30 a.m. to take care of last-minute details. By 7 a.m., the people in the wedding party have usually eaten breakfast, changed into their wedding clothes, and are waiting in the kitchen to greet the guests. Some 200 to 400 relatives, friends and church members are invited to the ceremony, which is held in the bride's home.

The 'Forgeher', or ushers (usually four married couples) will make sure each guest has a place on one of the long wooden benches in the meeting or church room of the home. At 8.30 a.m., the three-hour-long service begins. The congregation will sing hymns (without instrumental accompaniment), while the minister counsels the bride and groom in another part of the house. After the minister and the young couple return to the church room, a prayer, Scripture reading and sermon take place. Typically, the sermon is a very long one.

After the sermon is concluded, the minister asks the bride and groom to step forward from their seats with the rest of the congregation. Then he questions them about their marriage to be, which is similar to taking wedding vows. The minister then blesses the couple. After the blessing, other ordained men and the fathers of the couple may give testimony about marriage to the congregation. A final prayer draws the ceremony to a close.

That's when the festivities begin. In a flurry of activity, the women rush to the kitchen to get ready to serve dinner while the men set up tables in a U-shape around the walls of the living room. A corner of the table will be reserved for the bride and groom and the bridal party. This is an honoured place called the 'Eck', meaning corner. The tables are set at least twice during the meal, depending on how many guests were invited. The tables are laden with the 'roast' (roast chicken with bread stuffing), mashed potatoes, gravy, creamed celery, coleslaw, apple sauce, cherry pie, fruit salad, tapioca pudding, and bread, butter and jelly.

The bride sits on the groom's left, in the corner, the same way they will sit as man and wife in their buggy. The single women sit on the same side as the bride and the single men on that of the groom. The immediate family members sit at a long table in the kitchen, with both fathers seated at the head.

After dinner, the afternoon is spent visiting, playing games and matchmaking. Sometimes the bride will match unmarried boys and girls, who are over 16 years old, to sit together at the evening meal. The evening meal starts at 5.00 p.m. The parents of the bride and groom, and the older guests, are now seated at the main table and are the first to be served. The supper varies from the traditional noon meal. A typical menu might consist of stewed chicken, fried sweet potatoes, macaroni and cheese, peas, cold-cuts, pumpkin and lemon sponge pies, and cookies. The day usually winds to a close around 10.30 p.m.

Adapted from http://www.800padutch.com

53

TASK TIP

Descriptive compositions need to be shaped, just as narratives and arguments do, and in each passage above you can see that there is progression and structure. The first moves chronologically and spatially through a short time span and the increasing approach of the storm. The second develops by moving microscopically from the town to the factories to the workers in the factories, from buildings to people. The third moves from concrete measurements to an abstract concept. You can use telescopic structure, sweeping your eye across a panoramic view from left to right, or make the observer move closer to the object. A description often moves from the general to the specific, from what usually happens to what is happening on this particular occasion.

Descriptions are often written in the present tense, as in the third passage, to give the effect of immediacy or permanency, but even those written in the past tense need to create a sense of something taking place as the viewer observes it.

13 Discuss as a class the following questions about the account in Activity **12**.

a Who do you think the audience for this text might be, and what makes you think so?

b How does this passage differ in content from those in Activities **5**, **7** and **9**?

c What are the stylistic features of this passage?

14 You are going to write an informative account of an annual celebration or ceremony held in your country, town/village or school. First make notes of the chronological stages of the event, then add factual details to develop the notes into sentences and paragraphs. Write about 450 words, which could be a first draft for a coursework assignment.

15 Pretend that you are a sports commentator watching a match, race or individual performance of some kind (e.g. a high dive). Write a paragraph in the present tense commentating on what is happening. Read it to the class to evaluate how convincing your account sounds.

16 Read the brief account below of the last voyage of the ship *Mary Celeste*.

In the afternoon of 5th December 1872, Captain Morehouse, master of the **brig** *Dei Gratia*, in mid-Atlantic en route for Gibraltar, sighted another ship. He recognised it as the brig *Mary Celeste*, commanded by his old friend Captain Briggs, which had a month earlier been loading beside the *Dei Gratia* in New York. The sea was calm, the wind northerly and the sails of the *Mary Celeste* were set. Captain Morehouse signalled but received no reply. As the two vessels drew closer, Morehouse was puzzled by the haphazard way in which the brig was moving.

Captain Morehouse sent three of his men on board to investigate. They found the ship derelict but undamaged; there was no apparent reason for the crew's evacuation. The lifeboat, captain's **chronometer** and all the ship's papers were missing, with the exception of the logbook, whose last entry was dated ten days previously. Otherwise, everything was in good order, there were plentiful supplies and the cargo was intact.

Captain Morehouse took the *Mary Celeste* to Gibraltar as **salvage**, but of its master, his wife and child, and the ship's crew, no trace was ever found.

> **VOCABULARY**
>
> **brig:** two-masted sailing ship
> **chronometer:** time-keeping instrument used when navigating by the stars
> **salvage:** rescued parts of an abandoned ship or its cargo

17 What do you think happened aboard the *Mary Celeste*? Using your imagination, plan and write a first-person description, in the role of a surviving crew member, of the moment when you realised you would have to abandon ship. Include what you can see and hear, as well as your thoughts and feelings at the time. Read your piece, of about 300 words, to the class, who will vote on the most convincing and effective description.

18 Read the **monologue** account in the magazine article below.

A day in the life of Juana Oliveira

Juana Oliveira, 23, is a principal dancer with the Spanish National Ballet and the youngest ever to perform the leading role in Swan Lake. She is single and lives in Madrid with fellow dancers.

My alarm is set for 7:30, but sometimes I ignore it and drift back to sleep until 8:00, when my cat, Carlo, gets impatient for his breakfast and jumps on me. My breakfast consists of fruit juice, cereal and vitamin pills. I can walk to the rehearsal rooms but if it's raining or I am late, as is usually the case, I jump on a passing bus.

I get through a pair of practice shoes every two weeks, and tights don't last much longer. Class begins at 9:30 but before then we must do a fifteen-minute warm-up to avoid muscle strain. Class usually lasts about two hours and then we're free to do private practice for the rest of the day, but if there is a performance that evening, then there is another afternoon rehearsal as well. I enjoy the extra buzz of preparing for a performance and pushing my body to the limit.

I have wanted to be a ballerina since I was six years old, when my grandmother took me to see *Coppelia* on my birthday and I fell in love with the beautiful skill and grace of the dancers. It was a magic world and I cried at the end because I didn't want to go back to reality.

From then on I knew what I wanted to do and I started to keep a collection of ballet photographs and to go to every performance that it was possible to get to. I still love to watch other dancers and hope one day to go to Paris, Rome or London on a ballet tour. I started attending a specialist school in Barcelona when I was 11. My parents thought I would become too tall for a ballerina, and they were worried that the intensive training would interfere with my academic work.

Eventually they were reassured and stopped worrying about these things, and they are very proud of me now and visit often, bringing my little sister Maria to see me perform. My grandmother was very supportive from the beginning, but unfortunately she died last year. I miss her terribly but I hear her voice in my head when I am dancing, saying, 'Come on, Juana, you know you can do it!' There was a time when I was about 15 when I doubted my ability and resented the fact that I couldn't lead a normal life because of the need to practise in the evenings and at weekends. My friends always seemed to be doing things I couldn't join in with and I went through a lonely period.

Fortunately, my ballet teacher had faith in me and pushed me hard to prove that I had talent which shouldn't be wasted. I shall never forget the moment when I first performed in public at the age of 14, and when I danced my first leading role in *The Nutcracker* at 16. Because of that I was offered an audition for the Spanish National Ballet, and that led to a permanent contract with them. There were 40 girls at the audition, and I really didn't expect them to choose me. It was my dream come true.

At lunchtime a group of us go to a local salad bar, or buy sandwiches and fruit and have a picnic in the public gardens. Of course we have to be careful what we eat and if there's a performance in the evening we have very little. Throughout the day we nibble on nuts and dried fruit to keep our energy levels up, and we drink constantly to prevent dehydration. I think I must get through at least one and a half litres of milk per day – calcium is essential for dancers to keep their bones healthy – as well as many fruit juices and bottles of mineral water. After a performance I feel ravenously hungry and treat myself to fried potatoes and omelette when I get home, or a pizza backstage.

I unwind at the end of the day with Spanish music while I rub oil into my feet, which prevents blisters and hard skin. Carlo sits on my bed and watches me mischievously. He is just waking up as I fall asleep, after an exhausting but satisfying day.

'I have wanted to be a ballerina since I was six'

Part 3:
People and society

Unit 7: Reading Comprehension

This unit offers further practice in summary technique, sentence structuring, and in recognising and analysing how writers achieve effects. It looks at biographies, which are informative accounts.

> **KEY POINT**
>
> Summary style means selecting all the relevant material and expressing it:
>
> ■ as concisely as possible – without redundant words
>
> ■ without repeating ideas or words unnecessarily – using synonyms
>
> ■ choosing precise vocabulary – avoiding vague words
>
> ■ in formal register – without **colloquialisms** or abbreviations
>
> ■ in complex sentences – saving words and varying grammar structures.

1   Using the summary notes in the box below, write no more than 200 words about centenarians, including all the information. Think about the best way to group and then order the points before turning them into sentences. Use your own words as far as possible.

> ■ in the USA there are roughly 50,000 (1 in 8000)
> ■ 90% female
> ■ more than 90% reported good health until they reached their early 90s
> ■ about 15% live by themselves, completely independently
> ■ there is evidence that diet affects longevity
> ■ fastest-growing segment of US population – increasing 8% each year (1% for other age groups)
> ■ siblings of centenarians four times as likely to survive to age 90
> ■ longevity believed to be connected to optimistic view of life, which reduces body stress
> ■ female centenarians three times as likely to have had children when over age 40 as were women who lived to age 73.

2   Read the biographical fact sheet below.

1959	Born in Sudan. Her grandfather was a pioneer of women's education and her father was a newspaper editor and social reformer
1962	Family moved to London where her father worked for the BBC Arabic Service
1970	Attended Hornsey High School for Girls, London, taking A Levels in Russian, Latin and History
1978	Studied Philosophy, Politics and Economics at St Hilda's College, University of Oxford
1982	Broadcast journalist for Yorkshire Television
1988	Studied for MA in Middle East Politics and Anthropology at the School of Oriental and African Studies (SOAS), University of London
1988	First anchorperson to present the *ITV Morning News* television programme
1989	Co-presenter of *Channel Four News*
1998	Moved to BBC: hosted various news programmes, including *Hard Talk*
2009	Interviewed Sudan's President Omar Al-Bashir, the first serving head of state to be charged with war crimes
2009	Named International Television personality of the Year
2011	Appointed member of the Board of New College of the Humanities, London

She has also:

Founded African Medical Partnership Fund

Campaigned extensively for the rights of girls and women in traditional societies

Acted as Moderator of United Nations conferences

Acted as Adviser to the Foreign Policy Centre

Acted as a Council Member of the Overseas Development Institute

3   The facts about Zeinab Badawi are already in chronological order; now you need to decide which ones can be put together in the same sentence to create continuous writing and avoid using only list-like simple sentences. For example the facts about her education could be made into one complex sentence containing subordinating connectives and participle phrases. The grouping and ordering of information can be indicated on a copy of the fact sheet by using brackets and numbers.

4   Write a biographical summary for Zeinab Badawi up to 2011, using all the information in the fact sheet, in about 250 words. Remember to change at least some of the phrases into your own words.

5 Read the following mini-biography of a famous children's writer.

Roald Dahl

Home • **Roald Dahl** • **Create and Learn** • **Museum** • **Charity** • **Shop** • **Blog**

Roald Dahl was born on September 13, 1916, in Wales, UK, the son of Norwegian immigrants. His **colourful** experiences as a student in boarding schools were the inspiration for his books *Boy* and *Danny Champion of the World*.

Dahl became a writer during World War II, when he **recounted** in a short story his adventures as a fighter pilot. The story was bought by *The Saturday Evening Post* and a long, **illustrious** career was born. He travelled to East Africa, where he learnt Swahili, to Greece, and to the USA. While in New York he met and married in 1953 a film actress with whom he had five children. His interests were antiques, paintings and greyhounds.

After **establishing** himself as a writer for adults, Dahl began writing children's stories in 1960 while living in England with his family. His first two novels, *James and the Giant Peach* and *Charlie and the Chocolate Factory*, are now considered **classics** and both have been made into **blockbuster** films. He was the winner of England's two most **distinguished** literary awards, the Whitbread Prize and the Children's Book Award, and all of his works are **perennial** bestsellers. He did all his writing in a garden shed with six yellow pencils by his side.

Throughout his life, Dahl took great joy in hearing from his readers. He loved nothing more than to know he was entertaining them, as well as **instilling** in them a love of reading and books. Dahl once said, 'I know what children like.' His stories are proof positive that he was right, and are his **indelible legacy**. Roald Dahl passed away in Oxford, England, on November 23, 1990.

Adapted from www.roalddahl.com

6 **a** With a partner, agree synonyms for the **ten** words in bold in the text.

  b Find the words or phrases which show that the writer thinks that:

  i   Roald Dahl's life was unusual and exciting

  ii Roald Dahl's career was successful and worthwhile.

7 **a** With your partner, list the facts you have learned about Roald Dahl, in chronological order.

  b Look at the list you have made. What facts do readers appear to expect in a biography? (For example date of birth.)

8 Select the key points from your list in Activity 7b and in one complex sentence say who Roald Dahl was.

KEY POINT

The words *and*, *but*, *or* and *so* are connectives, but they link ideas through coordinatation (joining them equally) rather than subordination (making one more important than another). Therefore they do not enable you to form complex sentences, only compound ones. Overusing simple and compound sentences will make your writing sound repetitive, immature and imprecise. They also restrict your ability to vary your style, as these connectives are not normally used at the beginning of sentences, as subordinating connectives (e.g. *although*) can be. Complex sentences improve the style of nearly all kinds of continuous and directed writing, not only summaries.

9   Now look at the four sentences below. Which one is the best in terms of content and style? Why? Do the rest of the class agree? Is your sentence better than all of these? Can you improve your sentence?

a   Roald Dahl was born in Wales, where he wrote children's stories.

b   After establishing himself as a writer for adults, Roald Dahl began writing children's stories in 1960, his first two becoming classics.

c   Roald Dahl, who wrote children's stories with yellow pencils, was a fighter pilot during the Second World War.

d   Roald Dahl, who was born in 1916 in Wales of Norwegian descent, was a highly successful author of prize-winning children's fiction which inspired a love of reading.

10   How many of the following connectives do you regularly use in your writing?

when	(al)though	so that
who/m	if	as if
whose	before	as though
where	after	even if
which	since	even though
whoever	therefore	in order to
wherever	unless	in order that
while	because	as long as
whilst	until	as well as
whether	as	as soon as
whereas	for	as far as

11   Which of the connectives listed in Activity **10** do you never use? Write some sentences which show you know how to use them.

12   Join the simple sentences below into one complex sentence using some of the ways mentioned in the Task tip. Experiment with changing the order of the clauses.

Roald Dahl wanted his readers to be entertained by his books.
He wanted them to love reading.
He knew what children like.
He had five children.

TASK TIP

Over 30 connectives are available in English for joining clauses to form complex sentences. It can become a habit to use only a few of them, so to improve the variety and precision of your style learn to use as wide a range as possible. Sentence structures can also be varied by using:

■ present participle phrases (*Arriving* late, I missed the beginning; He didn't do it, *being* lazy)

■ past participle phrases (*Written* in 1916, the book was very popular; *Performed* in 1948, the play was well received)

■ participle phrases beginning with a preposition (*On discovering* the truth, I was horrified; *After having seen her*, I felt better).

Notice in Activity **11** the use of commas to separate the main and subordinate clauses. When the clause defines the preceding noun, it is called an **embedded clause** and the two parts should *not* be separated by a comma: *Zeinab Bedawi is a newsreader who is also a campaigner.*

There are three ways of ordering the clauses in a complex sentence:

■ main clause followed by subordinate clause, as in Activity **9a**

■ subordinate clause followed by main clause, as in Activity **9b**

■ subordinate clause embedded in main clause, as in Activities **9c** and **9d**.

13 Read the **obituary** below, as published on the Internet.

Cartoonist Charles Schulz dies at 77

Feb. 13, 2000

'Peanuts' creator Charles M. Schulz died on Saturday, turning his farewell note in Sunday papers into an **epitaph** for both a comic strip and its creator.

Schulz was 77, and died in his sleep at about 9:45 p.m. at his home in Santa Rosa, said his son, Craig. Only his wife, Jeannie, was with him when he died. Schulz was born in St. Paul, Minnesota, USA on Nov. 26, 1922.

He was diagnosed with colon cancer and suffered a series of small strokes during emergency abdominal surgery in November 1999. He announced his retirement a few weeks afterwards.

He studied art after he saw a 'Do you like to draw?' ad. His wildly popular 'Peanuts' made its debut on Oct. 2, 1950. The troubles of the 'little round-headed kid' and his pals eventually ran in more than 2,600 newspapers, reaching millions of readers in 75 countries. His last strip, appearing in Feb. 13 Sunday editions, showed Snoopy at his typewriter and other Peanuts regulars along with a 'Dear Friends' letter thanking his readers for their support.

Over the years, the Peanuts gang became a part of American popular culture, delivering gentle humor spiked with a child's-eye view of human **foibles**.

Sergio Aragones, a *Mad* magazine cartoonist and friend for more than 30 years, called Schulz 'a true cartoonist.' 'In a couple of centuries when people talk about American artists, he'll be the one of the very few remembered,' Aragones said. 'And when they talk about comic strips, probably his will be the only one ever mentioned.'

One of the most **endearing** qualities of 'Peanuts' was its constancy. The long-suffering Charlie Brown still faced misfortune with a mild 'Good grief!' Tart-tongued Lucy still handed out advice for a nickel. And Snoopy, Charlie

Brown's wise-but-weird beagle, still took the occasional flight of fancy back to the skies of World War I and his rivalry with the Red Baron.

Schulz was drafted into the Army in 1943 and sent to the European theater of war, although he saw little combat.

After the war, he did lettering for a church comic book, taught art and sold cartoons to *The Saturday Evening Post.* His first feature, 'Li'l Folks,' was developed for the *St. Paul Pioneer Press* in 1947. In 1950, it was sold to a **syndicate** and the name changed to 'Peanuts,' even though, he recalled later, he didn't much like the name.

Although he remained largely a private person, the strip brought Schulz international fame. He won the Reuben Award, comic art's highest honor, in 1955 and 1964. In 1978, he was named International Cartoonist of the Year, an award voted by 700 comic artists around the world. He was to have been honored with a lifetime achievement award on May 27 at the National Cartoonists Society **convention** in New York.

In his later years, he spent much of his time at his Redwood Empire Ice Arena in Santa Rosa, about 60 miles north of San Francisco, where he frequently played hockey or sipped coffee at the rink's Warm Puppy snack bar.

'Peanuts,' meanwhile, had remained an intensely personal effort. He had had a clause in his contract dictating the strip had to end with his death. While battling cancer, he **opted** to retire it right then, saying he wanted to focus on his health and family without the worry of a daily deadline.

'Why do musicians compose symphonies and poets write poems?' he once said. 'They do it because life wouldn't have any meaning for them if they didn't. That's why I draw cartoons. It's my life.'

TASK TIP

A prefix is a letter or group of letters added to the beginning of a word or word stem to add to or change its meaning. Prefixes are very common in English (the word *prefix* has a prefix!), and most of them come from Latin or Greek. Knowing their meanings helps you to guess unknown vocabulary and to spell words correctly – whether it is *hyper* ('above') or *hypo* ('below'), for example, or whether to use one *s* or two in *dis-satisfied*.

14 a Judging from the article, what is an obituary?

    b Where would you find one and who writes them?

    c What is its purpose and how does it differ from a biography?

    d Why would someone want to read one?

15 Explain the **six** words in bold in the passage.

16 a List the words in the passage which have prefixes.

    b Say what you think these prefixes mean.

    c Give examples of other words you know that begin with these prefixes.

17 With a partner, see how many prefixes and their meanings you can list in five minutes. The test for a prefix is whether a meaningful word stem remains after you remove it. Your teacher will collect the results on the board.

18 The material you select for a summary must relate to the exact wording of the question. Select material from the text in Activity **15** which you would use to summarise:

    a Charles Schulz's life and death

    b Charles Schulz's career and reputation as a cartoonist

    c the 'Peanuts' comic strip.

    Compare your choices with your partner's. Is there any information which you would use in more than one section?

19 Write a summary of the obituary, in not more than 250 words, which combines the material you selected for parts **a**, **b** and **c** of the previous activity.

    Remember to change the material into your own words, group it, order it and express it in complex sentences.

20 Read the two biographical extracts (Texts A and B) below about the 'mad monk' of Russia.

63

Text A

THE LIFE OF RASPUTIN

Gregory Rasputin was born on 10th January, 1869, into a Siberian peasant household. He spent much of his early adult life wandering Russia as a monk. In 1905, after the first Russian revolution, Rasputin infiltrated the imperial inner circle as the last in a long line of mystics. His miraculous ability to stem the bleeding of their haemophiliac son Alexei made him indispensable to the isolated, confused royal couple, Tsar Nicholas II and his wife, Alexandra. The support he provided, however, was as much emotional as practical.

Between 1905 and 1914, Rasputin charmed everyone he met, soothed the unhappy noblewomen who were his devotees and pursued an apparently sober holiness. When war arrived in 1914, the power-vacuum left by Russia's crushing defeats and Nicholas's absence at headquarters brought Rasputin almost supreme power alongside Alexandra. Monk and tsarina governed corruptly, unwisely appointing prime ministers and bishops, and even arranging the dismissal of the commander-in-chief, Grand Duke Nikolai. 'I'm a devil,' the monk admitted. 'I used to be holy.'

Everyone could see that the tsarina and the peasant-mystic Rasputin were driving Russia to ruin, hence the plot to kill him. The leader of the conspiracy was the fabulously wealthy Prince Felix Yussoupov, whose version of the events surrounding Rasputin's death was that he lured the monk to his palace, poisoned, shot and then tried to drown him, but still he would not die. What is certainly true is that when Rasputin's body was stuffed through the ice of the River Neva, he was still alive.

Adapted from an article by Simon Sebag Montefiore, *The Sunday Times*, 12th March 2000.

Text B

The Death of Rasputin

This is the first-person account of Dr Lazovert, a conspirator in the plot against Rasputin.

The story of Rasputin and his clique is well known. They sent the army to the trenches without food or arms, they left them there to be slaughtered, they betrayed Rumania and deceived the Allies, they almost succeeded in delivering Russia bodily to the Germans.

Rasputin, as a secret member of the Austrian Green Hand, had absolute power in Court. The Tsar was a nonentity, a kind of Hamlet, his only desire being to abdicate and escape the whole vile business.

Rasputin continued his life of vice, carousing and passion. The Grand Duchess reported these things to the Tsarina and was banished from Court for her pains.

This was the condition of affairs when we decided to kill this monster. Only five men participated in it. They were the Grand Duke Dmitri Pavlovich, Prince Yusupov, Vladimir Purishkevich, Captain Suhotine and myself.

Prince Yusupov's palace is a magnificent place on the Nevska. The great hall has six equal sides and in each hall is a heavy oaken door. One leads out into the gardens, the one opposite leads down a broad flight of marble stairs to the huge dining room, one to the library, etc.

At midnight the associates of the Prince concealed themselves while I entered the car and drove to the home of the monk. He admitted me in person.

Rasputin was in a gay mood. We drove rapidly to the home of the Prince and descended to the library, lighted only by a blazing log in the huge chimney-place. A small table was spread with cakes and rare wines – three kinds of the wine were poisoned and so were the cakes.

The monk threw himself into a chair, his humour expanding with the warmth of the room. He told of his successes, his plots, of the imminent success of the German arms and that the Kaiser would soon be seen in Petrograd.

At a proper moment he was offered the wine and the cakes. He drank the wine and devoured the cakes. Hours slipped by, but there was no sign that the poison had taken effect. The monk was even merrier than before.

We were seized with an insane dread that this man was inviolable, that he was superhuman, that he couldn't be killed. It was a frightful sensation. He glared at us with his black, black eyes as though he read our minds and would fool us.

And then after a time he rose and walked to the door. We were afraid that our work had been in vain. Suddenly, as he turned at the door, someone shot at him quickly.

With a frightful scream Rasputin whirled and fell, face down, on the floor.

[*The group leave the room to plan how to dispose of the body, but are interrupted.*]

Suddenly we heard a strange and unearthly sound behind the huge door that led into the library. The door was slowly pushed open, and there was Rasputin on his hands and knees [...]. With an amazing strength he sprang toward the door that led into the gardens, wrenched it open and passed out.

21 The two texts show two different ways of relaying the same information.

   a Which did you find more informative? Give examples.

   b Which did you find more entertaining? Give reasons.

   c What are the aim and audience of each text?

22 Express the following quotations from Text A in your own words. You may use a dictionary or thesaurus to help you.

   a *infiltrated the imperial inner circle*

   b *the power-vacuum left by Russia's crushing defeats*

   c *brought Rasputin almost supreme power alongside Alexandra*

As he seemed to be disappearing in the darkness, F. Purishkevich, who had been standing by, reached over and picked up an American-made automatic revolver and fired two shots swiftly into his retreating figure. We heard him fall with a groan, and later when we approached the body he was very still and cold and – dead.

We bundled him up in a sheet and carried him to the river's edge. Ice had formed, but we broke it and threw him in. The next day search was made for Rasputin, but no trace was found.

Urged on by the Tsarina, the police made frantic efforts, and finally ... the river was dragged and the body recovered.

I escaped from the country. Purishkevich also escaped. But Prince Yusupov was arrested and confined to the boundaries of his estate. He was later released because of the popular approval of our act.

Russia had been freed from the vilest tyrant in her history; and that is all.

(Stanislaus de Lazovert on the Assassination of Rasputin, 29th December 1916.)

From *Source Records of the Great War, Vol. V,* ed. Charles F. Horne, National Alumni 1923.

d   *were driving Russia to ruin*

e   *whose version of the events surrounding Rasputin's death*

23   In your own words, describe the characters of the Tsar and Tsarina as presented in Text B. Write a sentence for each.

24   Select words and phrases from Text B and explain how they convey:

   a   the character of Rasputin

   b   the dramatic nature of his death.

KEY POINT

When writing about writers' effects, you should select and quote words or phrases from parts of the passage. You need to demonstrate an awareness that language choices allow the reader to make inferences. Analyse your language choices to explain the feeling or atmosphere they convey through their connotations, e.g. '*sprang toward the door*' suggests a caged animal desperate to escape.

In addition to noting unusual, striking and powerful vocabulary and imagery, you can comment on relevant grammatical or literary features, such as irony, contrast, repetition, incongruity, short sentences (all of which occur in Text B above). You should not, however, simply list grammatical or literary terms; to show your understanding of how writers achieve effects you must make clear in full sentences – not as notes in a grid or column format – exactly what the writer's use of language evokes in the reader, in this particular case, and why.

25 What is the effect of each of the following five phrases in Text B?

   a *Hours slipped by*

   b *seized with an insane dread*

   c *his black, black eyes*

   d *his removal and obliteration*

   e *still and cold and – dead*

26 Select material from both extracts which would be relevant to a summary of Rasputin, divided into three sections:

   a his background and position at court

   b his character and behaviour

   c the circumstances and causes of his death.

List the points you have selected, then **collate**, group, sequence and change them into your own words.

➕ Further practice

   a Write a summary of Rasputin's life and death in about 250 words, using your plan from Activity **26**.

   b Research someone who interests you and write a biographical summary as a chronological list of notes. Read it to your class, leaving out the person's name, for your classmates to guess who it is.

   c As far as possible without repeating vocabulary, turn the following description of Garfield the cartoon cat into no more than 75 words, using only two sentences and reordering the information logically.

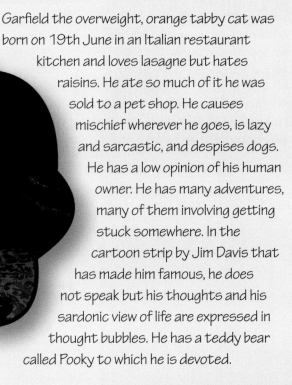

Garfield the overweight, orange tabby cat was born on 19th June in an Italian restaurant kitchen and loves lasagne but hates raisins. He ate so much of it he was sold to a pet shop. He causes mischief wherever he goes, is lazy and sarcastic, and despises dogs. He has a low opinion of his human owner. He has many adventures, many of them involving getting stuck somewhere. In the cartoon strip by Jim Davis that has made him famous, he does not speak but his thoughts and his sardonic view of life are expressed in thought bubbles. He has a teddy bear called Pooky to which he is devoted.

Unit 8: Response to Reading

This unit looks at and practises the features of different types of persuasive writing, including advertising. Further advice is given on choosing appropriate vocabulary, organising material and appealing to an audience.

1 Read the following extract from a holiday brochure.

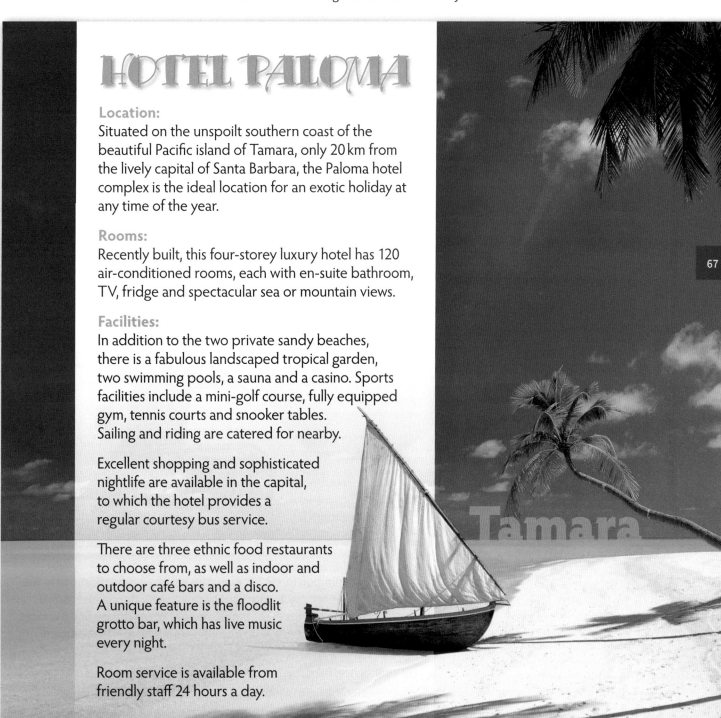

HOTEL PALOMA

Location:
Situated on the unspoilt southern coast of the beautiful Pacific island of Tamara, only 20 km from the lively capital of Santa Barbara, the Paloma hotel complex is the ideal location for an exotic holiday at any time of the year.

Rooms:
Recently built, this four-storey luxury hotel has 120 air-conditioned rooms, each with en-suite bathroom, TV, fridge and spectacular sea or mountain views.

Facilities:
In addition to the two private sandy beaches, there is a fabulous landscaped tropical garden, two swimming pools, a sauna and a casino. Sports facilities include a mini-golf course, fully equipped gym, tennis courts and snooker tables. Sailing and riding are catered for nearby.

Excellent shopping and sophisticated nightlife are available in the capital, to which the hotel provides a regular courtesy bus service.

There are three ethnic food restaurants to choose from, as well as indoor and outdoor café bars and a disco. A unique feature is the floodlit grotto bar, which has live music every night.

Room service is available from friendly staff 24 hours a day.

Tamara

TASK TIP

The style of a piece of writing is determined by its:

- aim – what is the purpose of the writing?
- speaker/writer – what kind of person is he or she claiming to be?
- audience – what do we know about their age, interests and expectations?
- vocabulary – how formal is the situation, relationship or subject?
- tone – what voice and mood are appropriate?
- sentence structure – should sentences be simple, compound or complex, or a mixture?

2 Find all the adjectives in the brochure extract. Discuss the following questions with your partner.

  a What associations do these words evoke?

  b Which emotions does the reader feel?

  c What kind of audience is the brochure targeting?

  d How does the choice of language make this passage effective as persuasive writing?

3 Imagine you recently stayed in the Hotel Paloma for a fortnight with your family, and you experienced a few problems. Consider the following questions and make a list of your complaints.

- Were all the facilities completed and adequate?
- Were you satisfied with your room? And the noise level?
- Did the beaches live up to expectation?
- How was the bus service, the room service, the service generally?
- How would you describe the catering?

Write a letter of complaint of about 350 words to the travel agency, Pegasus Travel, which arranged your holiday at the Hotel Paloma. Persuade the manager to give you a refund or another holiday as compensation. Refer to claims made in the brochure and be specific about your complaints.

4 One of the most common forms of persuasive writing is advertising, as in the holiday brochure in Activity **1**. With your partner, study the claims made by these three different brands of toothpaste below. Which do you find the most persuasive, and why? Can you write a one-line toothpaste ad that is even more persuasive?

  a For confidence, happiness and success, you need Flossy.

  b Your refreshing, bright, white smile says you are a Dentigel dazzler.

  c Healthy teeth and gums can be protected by regular brushing with scientifically proven, carbofluoride-rich Toothsome toothpaste.

KEY POINT

Persuasive writing aims to convince someone to do something for their own benefit or that of the writer. It is an important life skill and you may be required to demonstrate it in your responses to reading and writing exam questions or in coursework assignments.

To be effective, your response must be focused clearly on the purpose, give specific evidence, show awareness of the audience being targeted, and choose vocabulary to evoke the required emotional response (e.g. guilt, sympathy or fear). To be persuasive, be firm but polite; extreme language or abuse, even when complaining, can defeat your objective.

The **acronym** VARP (Voice, Audience, Register and Purpose) is a useful reminder of what needs to be considered when you are planning any piece of writing, but particularly when you need to be persuasive.

TASK TIP

Synonymous words have different strengths and **nuances**, and it is important in advertising, **propaganda**, and any other type of persuasive writing or speaking to pick exactly the right one to convey the connotation required to make the product or experience seem desirable. The wrong choice could create the wrong mood or conjure the wrong picture, and be off-putting to the reader or audience. It may even create an unintentional and inappropriate comic effect. Manufacturers have to be very careful to make sure that the name of their product has only positive connotations and will appeal to the intended market.

69

5 Decide in class which word in each pair is more emotionally powerful, and discuss the reasons in each case.

  a slaughter / kill
  b own / possess
  c house / home
  d attractive / beautiful
  e reluctantly / unwillingly
  f love / adore
  g phobia / fear
  h sad / sorrowful

Lunch

Mezze

The flavours of our home, presented as a generous spread of traditional Arabic savoury dishes including hommous, artichoke and mushroom salad, loubieh bil zeit and baba ghannouj, complemented by local garnishes.

Seafood selection

Fisherman's feast of premium smoked salmon and fresh dill-marinated prawns and scallops, served with avocado salsa.

Soup

A creamy home-style vegetable soup, served with sautéed peas.

Lamb noisette

Round tender lamb fillet, char-grilled and drizzled with lamb jus lié, served with roasted seasonal vegetables and creamy mashed potatoes.

Murg handi laziz

Succulent cubes of chicken cooked with Indian spices, accompanied by ginger-flavoured cauliflower and cumin-infused rice.

Prawn biryani

Classic Gulf dish of fresh prawns marinated and cooked in a broth with biryani rice and distinctive Arab spices, topped with fried onions and pine nuts.

Source: Emirates lunch menu, Dubai–Birmingham route.

6   With a partner, carry out the following activities:

   a   Underline the words in the menu above which have strong positive connotations.

   b   Explain why they have an appetising effect.

   c   List the words and phrases which are typically used in menus and explain why.

   d   Describe the **syntax** and style used in menus.

   e   Choose the dish which you think sounds the most desirable and explain why.

7   Here are two versions of a 'For Sale' advertisement for the same
    second-hand bicycle:

For Sale

Unique antique
bicycle in
reasonable
condition available
at a bargain price.

FOR SALE

Ancient bicycle,
in need of some
repair, going cheap.

TASK TIP

To avoid giving offence
personally or politically,
some types of writing
employ **euphemisms** (more
emotionally positive and
tactful, and less emotionally
negative and blunt, ways of
saying unpleasant things).
This is also a persuasive
device, as it directs attention
away from something which
may otherwise reduce the
reader's engagement with
or sympathetic response
to the text. The first advert
in Activity **7** contains
euphemisms (positive ways
of saying negative things).

a   With your partner, decide which advert is more likely to be successful, and
    why its vocabulary is more persuasive.

b   Write an advert of similar length for a possession, real or imaginary, which
    you wish to sell. Consider carefully your choice of vocabulary, grammar and
    order of information.

c   When you have finished drafting and improving it, read it to the class. Would
    they want to buy your object for sale?

8   With your partner:

a   Identify the euphemisms in the following sentences.

b   Think of more honest phrases that could replace them.

c   Discuss the differences of effect in each case.

    i   She is quite well built for someone her age.

    ii   The staff have voted to take industrial action.

    iii Unfortunately, there is no alternative: the dog must be put to sleep.

    iv   His behaviour has become somewhat eccentric lately.

    v   Our great nation will not be deterred by such a minor set-back.

9 Read the magazine article below about the pains and pleasures of becoming a jogger.

The joys of jogging

If you don't jog, jogging is impossible. When you do run for a couple of minutes – when needs really must – you find yourself beetroot in the face, slick with sweat and barely able to breathe. It is painful and undignified. And if in a two-minute dash to a bus stop you can be reduced to such a wreck, what would happen in four minutes? How can it be physically possible to run for 20, which is how long they say 'beginners' should jog for?

I jog now, very slowly, but very definitely and sort of regularly (in a random way), and I enjoy it. Or at least I feel smug and energetic and virtuous for having done it. I don't care that people tease me for shuffling along so slowly or for chatting so much while I shuffle. I am a jogging evangelist: I think it is the best exercise anyone can possibly do and I think that it has a more profound impact on your body than anything else you can do. If you want to get fit or lose weight there's nothing better.

There will always be people who preach the evils of jogging – we've all heard about dedicated joggers dropping dead at 50 – but in last week's British Medical Journal, Danish researchers said that their study of 20,000 people showed that regular joggers are far less likely to die prematurely than non-joggers.

So it's good for you. But how to start? I'll never forget how hard it was at the beginning: gazing up at an Everest of sweat and panting, and knowing that I would never be able to do it and that, even if I did, it would be terminally boring.

For the next three months or so, I stuck rigidly to my 'running' routine. I went to the gym three times a week, and I did my two minutes jogging, two minutes walking. … Slowly, it became easy. I stopped going red in the face and feeling uncomfortable. Then one morning a friend joined me at the gym. Not a fitness freak but an ordinary woman. I watched her jog, next to me, for 16 minutes. When I got off, at the end of my programme, she continued for another four minutes, but said nothing.

It was time to take the next step: continuous jogging. It had to be at walking pace, clearly, but continuous. First I did four minutes, then six minutes … much duller than two minutes. It was during this period that I took the big step off the running machine and into the outside. I went for 'a run' in the park. The first thing I noticed was how much faster the time went by outside. Within a month I was going for 20-minute runs.

Enter another friend, a regular jogger. He watched me run (walking alongside me) and said that there was no point in going so slowly. And so I speeded up so that I was running, although very slowly, rather than walking. A major breakthrough.

A marathon-running friend of my mother told me not long afterwards that I was doing fine. She said not to listen too much to macho male joggers anyway: the secret was – never run at a speed that it was uncomfortable to chat at.

About eight months into my new life, I returned to the gym for my fitness test. I was weighed and found that, without ever actually getting unpleasantly tired, I had lost about eight pounds. And just like that, I was a new woman. I could run for buses without breaking into a sweat.

My love of jogging is now about three years old and prone to dips. For the past four months, I've barely been out to the park once a week. But it doesn't matter. However long I leave between runs, I can still go out and jog for 20 minutes, and feel better for it. And the best of it is that not only is jogging free, but you can do it anywhere you find yourself.

Adapted from an article by Emily Wilson,
The Guardian, 12th September 2000.

TASK TIP

Response to reading tasks require you to use a range of vocabulary appropriate to the audience and context, which means that you must choose words not only for their explicit meaning but also for their associations, connotations and nuances (their implicit meanings) in order to evoke the desired response in the reader. Words are not neutral, and writers achieve their effects by choosing the best word for the purpose. For example, *teasing* is less strong than *mocking*, which is less strong than *bullying*, which is less strong than *threatening*, which is less strong than *menacing*, though you might find all of them together in a thesaurus.

TASK TIP

In order to be persuasive, you need to give facts and details to show that you are well informed about the topic. When aiming to elicit support from an audience, you need to convey your enthusiasm through vocabulary choice (especially emotive adjectives), a passionate tone and a style which is clear and authoritative.

10 Imagine you are the speaker in the article and you are trying to persuade a reluctant friend to join you in taking up jogging.

   a Scan the article, locating information which you would use to persuade your friend that jogging is a worthwhile activity.

   b Now scan it again, finding points which someone would use to explain why he or she is not keen on becoming a jogger.

11 Using the material you selected for Activity **10**, write about 350 words as a continuation of the following telephone conversation. Choose words which convey the appropriate attitude of enthusiasm or reluctance.

> Me: I've just got back from a good run and feel wonderful. You really ought to try jogging, you know. We could do it together.
>
> Friend: You must be joking! ...

12 Your gym has asked you to produce a single-sided A4 publicity **flyer** to hand out to its members, to explain:

   ■ the physical benefits of jogging
   ■ the mental benefits of jogging
   ■ the process of becoming a jogger.

   Write the text, using relevant material from the article and anything other relevant ideas that can be inferred from it. Use your own words and organise the points under appropriate topic headings.

13 In groups of three, imagine you are a student council committee trying to raise money for a new facility for your school (e.g. a swimming pool, sports hall, computer room or theatre).

   You are going to write a joint letter to former students of your school to persuade them to donate money towards the project.

   ■ What do you know about the audience?
   ■ What emotions do you want them to feel towards the school?
   ■ What would be an appropriate tone and style to use in the letter?

   First plan the structure and content of your letter, making notes on what you would put into each section. Write your letter, of about 350 words. One of you can read it out to the class, who can vote on the project they feel most persuaded to support.

73

KEY POINT

If you are given guidance about what to include in an answer, make sure you follow it. (If the question includes bullet points, use them as the basis for planning and structuring your response.) This ensures that you don't leave out anything essential, and that your answer is well organised and of an appropriate length.

14 Read the article and statistics below on the ages for young people beginning to drive in various countries.

Text A

Great news, Dad. Now I'm 16, the law says I can drive.

Would you let your 16-year-old get behind the wheel of a car? That's the question parents in the UK will be asking from this weekend, when a change in the law cuts the age at which youngsters can hit the road in a four-wheeled vehicle to the lowest level since the licensing of drivers began in 1903.

The change means youngsters will be able to throw their textbooks in the boot, turn on the stereo and pick up a friend on the way to school. [...]The vehicles they can drive are technically quadricycles and have a top speed of 45 kph, but they look like a conventional car outside and offer the comforts of one inside, including dryness and warmth.

The new law is worrying road safety charities, which say young people already account for too many casualties and that reducing the age at which they can go on the road could lead to an increase, especially as when there are two of them in a car, they tend to show off, because they feel invincible at that age.

Manufacturers argue that being surrounded by a metal box gives young drivers protection that they don't have on a bicycle or moped. But in America, where teenagers are allowed to drive a conventional car from the age of 16 in most states, accident figures show that the younger the driver the more likely they are to be involved in an accident, and risk is highest at ages 16–17, because of their immaturity combined with driving inexperience.

From an article by Dominic Tobin, *The Sunday Times*, 20th January 2013.

Text B

Minimum driving ages around the world

Region	Age
North, West and Southern Africa	18 – except Algeria
Canada and USA	16 – 14 in some states
Central America	18 – except Guatemala, Panama, Bahamas, Puerto Rico, Tridad and Tobago
South America	18 – except Columbia
West Asia	18 – except Israel (16 yrs 9 months) and Saudi Arabia, where women are banned from driving
South Asia and East Asia	18 – except Nepal and Philippines (16) and Malaysia (17)
Europe and Eastern Europe	18 – except Gibraltar (19) and UK, Hungary, Iceland, Channel Islands and Kosovo (17) and Isle of Man (16)
Australasia	varies by state between 16 and 18 in Australia, Fiji 17, New Zealand 16 ½

15 Select the arguments from Text A which are for and against the reduction of the driving age to 16, and put them in two columns.

16 a Summarise in no more than 75 words the information provided in the grid in Text B, beginning:

In the majority of countries, the minimum driving age is …

    b What can you infer from the Text B about:

      i driving on an island

      ii driving in an underpopulated country?

    c What is implied by the additional information that several countries have

      i a lower driving age if supervised by a parent

      ii a higher driving age for a commercial vehicle?

17 Imagine you are about to turn 16 and believe you should be allowed to drive, even though it is not legal in your country. Write a letter to a national newspaper putting forward your case. Use facts and inferred ideas from the texts in Activity **14** to present a persuasive case.

18 Read the ending of a short story below. The narrator is a 14-year-old boy in India who loves playing cricket with his friend Viraf, whose father is ill. His own father is unemployed and the narrator has to pluck out his grey hairs to make him look younger and more likely to get a job.

No one saw us as we tiptoed outside; they were absorbed in whatever the discussion was about.

'*Puppa* is very sick,' whispered Viraf as we passed the sickroom. I stopped and looked inside. It was dark. The smell of sickness and medicines made it stink like the waiting room of Dr Sidhwa's dispensary. Viraf's father was in bed, lying on his back, with a tube through his nose. There was a long needle stuck into his right arm, and it <u>glinted cruelly in a thin shaft of sunlight that had suddenly slunk inside the darkened room</u>. I shivered. The needle was connected by a tube to a large bottle which hung upside down from a dark metal stand towering over the bed. [...] <u>Supine, his rotundity had spread into a flatness denying his huge bulk</u>. I remembered calling Viraf a cry-baby, and my face flushed with shame. I swore I would apologise. [...]

My eyes fixed on the stone-grey face of Viraf's father, I backed out of the sickroom, unseen. The hallway was empty. Viraf was waiting for me in the back room with the boards for Ludo and Snakes-and-Ladders. But I sneaked through the veranda and down the stairs without a word.

The compound was flooded in sunshine as I returned to the other end. On the way I passed the three white stumps we had once chalked on the compound wall's black stone. [...]

Daddy was still reading *The Times*, at the dining-table. [...] The tweezers were lying on the table. I picked them up. They glinted pitilessly, like that long needle in Viraf's father. I dropped them with a shudder, and they clattered against the table.

Daddy put down the newspaper and removed his glasses. He rubbed his eyes, then went to the bathroom. How tired he looked, and how his shoulders drooped; his gait lacked confidence, and I'd never noticed that before. He did not speak to me even though I was praying hard that he would. Something inside me grew heavy, and I tried to swallow, to dissolve the heaviness in saliva, but swallowing wasn't easy either; the heaviness was blocking my throat. I heard the sound of running water. Daddy was

19 a Explain in your own words the three phrases underlined in the passage.

 b Choose words and phrases that you found powerful and evocative, and explain why.

 c Contribute to a class discussion of the message of the end of the story, using quotations to support your view.

> **❝ VOCABULARY**
>
> **mamaiji:** grandmother
> **kustis:** girdles
> **Primus:** portable paraffin cooking stove

preparing to shave. I wanted to go and watch him, talk to him, laugh with him at the funny faces he made to get at all the tricky places with the razor, especially the cleft in his chin.

Instead, I threw myself on the bed. I felt like crying, and buried my face in the pillow. I wanted to cry for the way I had treated Viraf, and for his sick father with the long, cold needle in his arm and his rasping breath; for **Mamaiji** and her tired, darkened eyes spinning thread for our **kustis**, and for Mummy growing old in the dingy kitchen smelling of kerosene, where the **Primus** roared and her dreams were extinguished; I wanted to weep for myself, for not being able to hug Daddy when I wanted to, and for not ever saying thank you for cricket in the morning, and pigeons and bicycles and dreams; and for all the white hairs I was powerless to stop.

From 'Of White Hairs and Cricket' in *Stories of Ourselves*, by Rohinton Mistry.

20 Plan and write a response to the passage in the form of a journal entry by the narrator, using your own words. Write about 300 words. Your response should include your thoughts and feelings about the following characters and their situation:

- Viraf's father
- Viraf
- your father.

21 You are going to work on a charity project in groups of four or five. (Your teacher may monitor your group discussions for speaking and listening assessments.)

First read the letter.

Aid to Africa International Constitution Square Frankfurt

Caught in the conflict.
Struggling to survive the burning heat.
Together we can help them win.

Dear Supporter,

We can't help but be moved by the pictures of human suffering in the conflict in Darfur, Sudan. But there are just as many innocent victims of civil war in neighbouring countries. Across the whole of eastern Africa, in Eritrea, Ethiopia and Chad, thousands of innocent families have escaped from the fierce fighting only to face a new risk from the deadly combination of boiling heat, starvation and disease.

Charuni's refugee family is typical of many. Since last June they have lived in a damp and unsanitary refugee camp outside the town of Al Khartum. Now as summer tightens its deadly grip, her family of 13 huddle together for comfort and try to find shade wearing the rags their clothing has become.

But there are refugees who don't even have a canvas roof over their heads. Many fleeing families are spending the baking summer months in the open, under trees in the bush, in hillside caves, where they must brave the fierce, searing winds, swirling dust, and cold nights, and where daytime temperatures reach above 40 degrees.

To make matters worse, disrupted food supplies often mean that people haven't eaten properly for a year or more. Many women have lost as much as 16 kg and malnutrition means children are becoming vulnerable to the slightest infection.

In the middle of summer, safe drinking water and protective sheeting could make the difference between life and death.

Homeless, hungry and exhausted, their spirit sapped by the horrors of war, thousands of families are struggling to survive.

Unless they get help, the added burden of drought may prove too much for these families and many will not live to see the rainy season.

A2A is already working hard to prevent that happening. We are the only agency to get through the front lines and deliver aid to where it's most needed. We are already shipping tents, water and sanitation kits to UN refugee camps. Where necessary, we charter helicopters to get supplies to villages in remote areas. But as summer drags on, we desperately need your help to send more supplies of Survival Packs to frightened and starving families.

*An **A2A** food parcel feeds a family for a month.*

A2A Survival Packs contain the best combination of food, liquids, and sheeting needed to get a refugee family through the summer.

A $20 gift from you would fill a Pack with enough supplies to feed a family of four for a month. $60 would buy a Pack to keep a family of five shaded and hydrated throughout the summer. And $100 would provide enough canvas for 10 temporary shelters.

As summer scorches on, these families are in a race against time. Hundreds of innocent and vulnerable people are depending on **A2A** Summer Survival Packs. <u>The sooner you help us, the sooner we can act, the better their chances of survival</u>.

*Emergency **A2A** supplies mean refugee children can be immunised against disease.*

A2A will not stand by and let summer sap away the strength of families who have already been through so much. Please send your gift today and help us deliver the Summer Survival Packs and give thousands of families a fighting chance to see another autumn in Eastern Africa.

Yours faithfully,

Dino Karides

International Aid Department

This is a fictional letter written by the Coursebook author.

TASK TIP

For your answer to Activity 23 you have probably chosen the battle metaphors and clichés, and the words to do with heat and pain, which are all intended to make the reader feel pity. The personification of summer as a bringer of disease, starvation and death intensifies the effect of it being an even greater enemy than the war the refugees are fleeing from. The contrast between them and us, and the emphasis on the passing of time, create a feeling of guilt and a sense of urgency. These are techniques you can use in your own persuasive writing.

22 What is a 'charity'?

   a List the kinds of things which charities raise money for.

   b List the names of as many official international charities as you can think of.

   c Discuss why you think charities need to exist.

23 Choose the words and phrases in this letter which you find the most persuasive. Discuss why do you think the chosen words have this effect.

24 What exactly is the purpose of the letter? Discuss in your group.

    a the kinds of material which are included

    b whether the content is fact or opinion, or both

    c why you think statistics and numbers are used.

25 Think about the charity's name and symbol. Why are they memorable?

    a Draw other charity symbols or **logos** you can think of (e.g. the candle and barbed wire for Amnesty International).

    b Look back at and discuss the names you listed in Activity **22b**.

    c What can you conclude about effective names and symbols?

26 Imagine your group is going to establish a new charity. What do you feel strongly about, as a local, national or international concern? Discuss and agree on a good cause.

    a Choose a name for your charity. How can you make it memorable?

    b Design a symbol or logo. How can you make it instantly recognisable?

27 Your charity is going to send an appeal letter to the general public. First study the appeal letter in Activity **21** again, this time focusing on structure and style.

    a What are the different stages of the letter?

    b How would you describe the adjectives used?

    c What is the effect of the use of lists?

    d Why does it begin *Dear Supporter*?

    e What effect do the subject pronouns *we*, *you* and *they* have?

    f Where and why is repetition used?

    g Why do you think the word *family* is mentioned so often?

    h What can you say about paragraph length and sentence structure?

    i Are the tone and style formal or informal, or both?

28 Look at the visual features and the layout of the Aid to Africa letter.

    a Which parts stand out most? Why?

    b List the layout and graphic devices used in the letter.

TASK TIP

Layout is an aspect of the art of persuasion. A persuasive text for a mass audience may fail if it is unattractive or too densely arranged on the page (one of the reasons why your writing should always be paragraphed). When you are producing coursework on a keyboard, the following devices can be used to break up text blocks and give variety and visual appeal:

- coloured type
- capitals
- captions
- font size changes
- boxes and shading
- bold type
- underlining
- asterisks
- bullets
- headings and sub-headings
- wide margins
- blank lines.

But remember: it is your English language skills which are being assessed, not your artistic or technological ability!

TASK TIP

You may already know enough between you about your chosen cause and can pool your knowledge. If not, reference books, internet sites, magazine articles or newspapers can be used as resources for information and illustrations. Although you have made up your own charity name, there are probably some real charities in existence which do similar work.

29 Divide responsibilities for different areas or aspects of your charity's appeal letter among the members of the group. Each person should research, plan and present ideas to the rest of the group for approval.

The responsibilities could be divided as follows:

- illustrations and captions
- structure and layout design
- factual and statistical research
- selection and writing of content
- proofreading and editing.

30 Draft and finalise the appeal letter on a computer, combining the contributions of each group member. Check that you have used the ideas in and answers to Activities **22–28**, and that you have included a range of types, colours and layout features, as well as illustrations. Display your letters in the classroom.

➕ Further practice

a Develop your appeal letter into a script to be used as a voice-over for a television appeal broadcast. The speech must be exactly three minutes long to fit the slot. You may need to reorder and rephrase some of the material in the letter.

You can read your script to the class and they can vote for the charity they feel persuaded to donate money to as a result of the broadcasts.

b You would really like to go on holiday with some friends this year, instead of with your family as usual. List and order the facts and points you would use to persuade your parents to let you go, and anticipate their objections. Write a **dialogue** of about 350 words between you and a parent, in which you succeed in persuading them.

c You are going to start and run a club at your school. Write a handout to pass round and display on notice boards to persuade students to join. Tell them the club's name, what you propose it will do and why they should want to join. Write about 300 words.

Unit 9: Continuous Writing

This unit introduces and gives practice in narrative writing skills, focusing on plot, pace and structure, setting and atmosphere, openings and endings.

1 Read the extract from an autobiography below. It concerns a young man who left home in rural England in 1936 to fight in the Spanish Civil War.

The stooping figure of my mother, waist-deep in the grass and caught there like a piece of sheep's wool, was the last I saw of my country home as I left it to discover the world. She stood old and bent at the top of the bank, silently watching me go, one gnarled red hand raised in farewell and blessing, not questioning why I went. At the bend of the road I looked back again and saw the gold light die behind her; then I turned the corner, passed the village school, and closed that part of my life for ever.

It was a bright Sunday morning in early June, the right time to be leaving home. I was nineteen years old, still soft at the edges, but with a confident belief in good fortune. I carried a small rolled-up tent, a violin in a blanket, a change of clothes and a tin of treacle biscuits. As I left home that morning and walked away from the sleeping village, it never occurred to me that others had done this before me.

And now I was on my journey, in a pair of thick boots and with a hazel stick in my hand. Naturally, I was going to London, which lay a hundred miles to the east; and it seemed equally obvious that I should go on foot. But first, as I'd never yet seen the sea, I thought I'd walk to the coast and find it. I had all the summer and all time to spend.

From *As I Walked Out One Midsummer Morning*, by Laurie Lee.

2 With a partner, identify and comment on the effects of the imagery, details and adjectives which have been used to create:

a setting

b atmosphere

c mood (feelings evoked by the passage).

3 a Plan the first chapter of your autobiography. Think about where it would be set, what event it would deal with, and what mood you want it to have.

b Write the first two paragraphs to establish the setting and the occasion (as in the passage in Activity 1).

TASK TIP

Using your personal experience as the basis for a narrative exam composition or coursework piece will help your writing to be original and authentic, and make it easier for you to think of a situation to write about. You can also use events which happened to someone else, either in reality or in a book or film. Because the aim of narrative is to amuse, entertain or frighten – not to inform or tell the truth – you can exaggerate, adapt, add or remove things, and do whatever will make your story more engaging.

KEY POINT

Narrative is usually written in the past tense, the natural mode for relating something which has already happened, and candidates who begin writing in the present tense often forget and switch to the past tense after a few paragraphs. Narrative must be built around an event or series of events but is made distinctive by including other elements:

- reflections (thoughts and attitudes)
- emotions (feelings and memories)
- descriptions (of people and places).

You must not only tell an interesting story in order to engage the reader, but also create a setting and an atmosphere for it. The reader needs a sense of time, place and weather to be able to picture the scene. Whether your narrative is serious or amusing, sad or cheerful, will depend on how you choose your vocabulary and what descriptive details you give, as these create mood.

4 Read the following extract from a ghost story. (Spider is a dog.)

After a while, I heard the odd sound again. It seemed to be coming from along the passage to my left, at the far end. But it was still quite impossible to identify. Very cautiously, listening, hardly breathing, I ventured a few steps in that direction. Spider went ahead of me. The passage led only to three other bedrooms on either side and, one by one, regaining my nerve as I went, I opened them and looked inside each one. Nothing, only heavy old furniture and empty unmade beds and, in the rooms at the back of the house, moonlight. Down below me on the ground floor of the house, silence, a seething, blanketing, almost tangible silence, and a musty darkness, thick as felt.

And then I reached the door at the very end of the passage. Spider was there before me and her body, as she sniffed beneath it, went rigid, her growling grew louder. I put my hand on her collar, stroked the rough, short hair, as much for my own reassurance as for hers. I could feel the tension in her limbs and body and it answered to my own.

This was the door without a keyhole, which I had been unable to open on my first visit to Eel Marsh House. I had no idea what was beyond it. Except the sound.

Adapted from *The Woman in Black*, by Susan Hill.

5 Working with a partner:

a List the words and phrases in the extract in Activity **4** which create an atmosphere of fear and an expectation that something unpleasant is about to happen.

b Explain why they have this effect.

c Study the sentence structuring. How does the **syntax** contribute to the atmosphere?

TASK TIP

First-person narratives have the advantage of sounding like genuine experience, but they are limited to one viewpoint, and by the knowledge that the narrator must have survived in order to be telling the tale, which can reduce the tension (a first-person account cannot end with *And then I died*.) So before you begin writing a narrative, think carefully about how you want it to end.

One or two events and two or three characters are sufficient for a short story, and the time period which can be effectively covered is usually only a day or two. It is not possible to fit more into the time and space available, and trying to fit too much into a narrative spoils the pace, **climax** and creation of suspense, and reduces the amount of necessary descriptive detail to convey character and setting.

6 Read the extract below from a short story set in South Africa, in which an elderly man is trying to escape from a gang of youths who intend to steal his money.

So trapped was he that he was filled suddenly with strength and anger, and he ran towards the wasteland swinging his heavy stick. In the darkness a form loomed up at him, and he swung at it, and heard it give a cry of pain. Then he plunged blindly into the wilderness of wire and iron and the bodies of old cars.

Something caught him by the leg, and he brought his stick crashing down on it, but it was no man, only some knife-edged piece of iron. He was sobbing and out of breath but he pushed on into the waste, while behind him they pushed on also, knocking against the old iron bodies and kicking against tins and buckets. He fell into some grotesque shape of wire; it was barbed and tore at his clothes and flesh. Then it held him, so that it seemed to him that death must be near, and having no other hope, he cried out, 'Help, help me!' in what should have been a great voice, but was voiceless and gasping. He tore at the wire, and it tore at him too, ripping his face and his hands.

From 'The Wasteland', by Alan Paton.

7 **a** Select from the above extract all the words and short phrases which convey a feeling of danger or pain.

 b Write comments to explain the meanings and connotations of these words (for example, *barbed* means pointed and with the word *wire* it makes us think of places that people are forbidden to enter or leave.)

8 Discuss with your partner what features the two previous extracts have in common, and how they differ. Consider the following:

- narrator
- atmosphere
- setting
- sense of a presence
- references to noise or silence

- use of paragraphing
- use of adjectives and adverbs
- choice of verbs
- sentence structure
- pace (speed of events).

TASK TIP

Narrative writing can create tension with sinister adjectives and adverbs, and horror can be evoked by the use of violent verbs, especially those which give objects a human power. Suspense can be created by slowing the pace, so that there is a sense of waiting and nothing actually happens for a while (see Activity **4**), whereas panic is created by the opposite technique of using a lot of quick actions in a short time to suggest uncontrolled speed (as in Activity **6**). Paragraph breaks, sentence length and punctuation all affect the rhythm and tension of a piece of writing.

Notice that in both passages there is an unknown *it*; something mysterious arouses curiosity and this is often more frightening than a known and visible enemy. Many stories are spoiled by unconvincing gory description, and some of the best narratives are understated or leave something unexplained for the reader to think about.

9   This extract from an autobiography is about the capture of a poisonous snake which has got into a family home in Tanzania, Africa. The narrator and house owner are watching through the window what happens inside the room.

The snake-man went up the steps first and he made absolutely no sound at all with his feet. He moved soft and catlike onto the veranda and straight through the front door and then he quickly but very quietly closed the door behind him.

The living room was simple and ordinary, coconut matting on the floor, a red sofa, a coffee table and a couple of armchairs. The dog was sprawled on the matting under the coffee table, a large Airedale with curly brown and black hair. He was stone dead.

The snake-man was standing absolutely still just inside the door of the living room. The brown sack was now slung over his left shoulder and he was grasping the long pole with both hands, holding it out in front of him, parallel to the ground. I couldn't see the snake. I didn't think the snake-man had seen it yet either.

A minute went by ... two minutes ... three ... four ... five. Nobody moved. There was death in that room. The air was heavy with death and the snake-man stood as motionless as a pillar of stone, with the long rod held out in front of him.

And still he waited. Another minute ... and another ... and another. And now I saw the snake-man beginning to bend his knees. Very slowly he bent his knees until he was almost squatting on the floor, and from that position he tried to peer under the sofa and the armchairs. And still it didn't look as though he was seeing anything. Slowly he straightened his legs again, and then his head began to swivel around the room. Over to the right, in the far corner, a staircase led up to the floor above. The snake-man looked at the stairs, and I knew very well what was going through his head.

Quite abruptly, he took one step forward and stopped. Nothing happened.

A moment later I caught sight of the snake. It was lying full-length along the skirting of the right-hand wall, but hidden from the snake-man's view by the back of the sofa. It lay there like a long, beautiful, deadly shaft of green glass, quite motionless, perhaps asleep. It was facing away from us who were at the window, with its small triangular head resting on the matting near the foot of the stairs.

I nudged Fuller and whispered, 'It's over there against the wall.' I pointed and Fuller saw the snake. At once,

he started waving both hands, palms outward, back and forth across the window, hoping to get the snake-man's attention. The snake-man didn't see him. Very softly, Fuller said, 'Pssst!' and the snake-man looked up sharply. Fuller pointed. The snake-man understood and gave a nod.

Now the snake-man began working his way very very slowly to the back wall of the room so as to get a view of the snake behind the sofa. He never walked on his toes as you or I would have done. His feet remained flat on the ground all the time. The cowhide boots were like moccasins, with neither soles nor heels. Gradually, he worked his way over to the back wall, and from there he was able to see at least the head and two or three feet of the snake itself.

But the snake also saw him. With a movement so fast it was invisible, the snake's head came up about two feet off the floor and the front of the body arched backwards, ready to strike. Almost simultaneously, it bunched its whole body into a series of curves, ready to flash forward.

The snake-man was just a bit too far away from the snake to reach it with the end of his pole. He waited, staring at the snake, and the snake stared back at him with two small malevolent black eyes.

Then the snake-man started speaking to the snake. 'Come along, my pretty,' he whispered in a soft wheedling voice. 'There's a good boy. Nobody's going to hurt you. Nobody's going to harm you, my pretty little thing. Just lie still and relax ...' He took a step forward toward the snake, holding the pole out in front of him.

What the snake did next was so fast that the whole movement couldn't have taken more than a hundredth of a second, like the flick of a camera shutter. There was a green flash as the snake darted forward at least ten feet and struck at the snakeman's leg. Nobody could have got out of the way of that one. I heard the snake's head strike against the thick cowhide boot with a sharp little crack, and then at once the head was back in that same deadly backward-curving position, ready to strike again.

'There's a good boy,' the snake-man said softly. 'There's a clever boy. There's a lovely fellow. You mustn't get excited. Keep calm and everything's going to be all right.' As he was speaking, he was slowly lowering the end of the pole until the forked prongs were about twelve inches above the middle of the snake's body. 'There's a lovely fellow,' he whispered. 'There's a good kind little chap. Keep still now, my beauty. Keep still, my pretty. Keep quite still. Daddy's not going to hurt you.'

I could see a thin dark trickle of venom running down the snake-man's right boot where the snake had struck.

The snake, head raised and arcing backwards, was as tense as a tight-wound spring and ready to strike again. 'Keep still, my lovely,' the snake-man whispered. 'Don't move now. Keep still. No one's going to hurt you.'

Then wham, the rubber prongs came down right across the snake's body, about midway along its length, and pinned it to the floor. All I could see was a green blur as the snake thrashed around furiously in an effort to free itself. But the snake-man kept up the pressure on the prongs and the snake was trapped.

What happens next? I wondered. There was no way he could catch hold of that madly twisting flailing length of green muscle with his hands, and even if he could have done so, the head would surely have flashed around and bitten him in the face.

Holding the very end of the eight-foot pole, the snake-man began to work his way round the room until he was at the tail end of the snake. Then, in spite of the flailing and the thrashing, he started pushing the prongs forward along the snake's body toward the head. Very very slowly he did it, pushing the rubber prongs forward over the

snake's flailing body, keeping the snake pinned down all the time and pushing, pushing, pushing the long wooden rod forward millimetre by millimetre. It was a fascinating and frightening thing to watch, the little man with white eyebrows and black hair carefully manipulating his long implement and sliding the fork ever so slowly along the length of the twisting snake toward the head. The snake's body was thumping against the coconut matting with such a noise that if you had been upstairs you might have thought two big men were wrestling on the floor.

Then at last the prongs were right behind the head itself, pinning it down, and at that point the snake-man reached forward with one gloved hand and grasped the snake very firmly by the neck. He threw away the pole. He took the sack off his shoulder with his free hand. He lifted the great, still twisting length of the deadly green snake and pushed the head into the sack. Then he let go the head and bundled the rest of the creature in and closed the sack. The sack started jumping about as though there were fifty angry rats inside it, but the snake-man was now totally relaxed and he held the sack casually in one hand as if it contained no more than a few pounds of potatoes. He stooped and picked up his pole from the floor, then he turned and looked toward the window where we were peering in.

'Pity about the dog,' he said. 'You'd better get it out of the way before the children see it.'

From 'The Green Mamba' in *Going Solo*, by Roald Dahl, 1986.

10 Work in small groups on a copy of the passage in Activity 9. Prepare answers to the following questions for a class discussion.

a Where does the pace change in the passage? Mark the places where you think the action is speeding up or slowing down.

b What do you think would be the duration in reality of the actions narrated from *But the snake also saw him* to *the snake was trapped*, and how does this compare to the time it takes to read it?

c How would the narrative have been different in content and effect on the reader if the entire incident had been described briefly in one paragraph?

d List the devices used to create pace in the passage, both fast and slow.

e Identify the climax of the passage and explain how you know.

f Describe the structure of the passage in the form of a diagram.

g Why are we told at the beginning of the passage that the dog is dead, and why is it mentioned again at the end?

h What is the effect of the double narration (i.e. a first-person observer of an action carried out by a third person)?

i If you had to make cuts in the passage to reduce its length by half but still retain the essential features, what would you remove? Use square brackets to edit the text.

11 Read aloud as a class the poem below by an American poet.

Stopping by Woods on a Snowy Evening

Whose woods these are I think I know.
His house is in the village, though;
He will not see me stopping here
To watch his woods fill up with snow.

My little horse must think it queer
To stop without a farmhouse near
Between the woods and frozen lake
The darkest evening of the year.

He gives his harness bells a shake
To ask if there is some mistake
The only other sound's the sweep
Of easy wind and downy flake.

The woods are lovely, dark, and deep,
But I have promises to keep,
And miles to go before I sleep,
And miles to go before I sleep.

By Robert Frost.

87

12 The poem describes the setting and atmosphere, but the event and characters have been left unspecified and mysterious.

a Think of a plot which would fit the poem's mood.

b Then write the first paragraph of the story. Share it with the rest of the class, and vote for the opening which would most make the reader want to read on.

88

TASK TIP

Sometimes in narratives a short sentence – or even a non-sentence – can be dramatically effective, especially at the beginning or end, or at a climactic moment. Remember, however, that complex sentences are generally the best way of expressing yourself with variety and concision, and of proving your command of English. Avoid beginning every sentence with its subject, or using *and then*, which is monotonous and unnecessary in chronological writing. In an exam, a continuous writing response needs a range of appropriate vocabulary, so try not to repeat words, and aim to use ambitious but accurate language.

13 Most narrative openings fall into one of six categories:

a middle of the action

b setting the scene/atmosphere

c introducing the main character

d middle of the dialogue

e shock (unexpected)

f intrigue (mystery).

Which type did you use in Activity **12**?

14 Write one of each of the six types of opening sentence listed in Activity **13**, for a composition entitled *The secret room*. Show your sentences to your partner, who will choose the best.

15 Now write the final sentence for your story. How would you describe the type of ending you have used?

TASK TIP

An anticlimactic, predictable or overused ending (such as *and then I woke up*) will disappoint the reader and weaken the effectiveness of your narrative. A satisfying ending can be:

■ a 'cliffhanger' (*But just at that moment, the phone rang.*)

■ a short piece of humorous, dramatic or ironic direct speech (*There's something I didn't tell you: the cat can talk!*)

■ an unexpected/ironic twist (*The Wasteland* ends with the man discovering that his attacker, whom he has killed in self-defence, was his own son)

■ a return to the beginning (repeating the first sentence or referring to the event which began the story)

■ 'happily-ever-after' (*Shortly afterwards, they agreed to get married.*)

■ an open ending (*No one knows if they ever learned the truth.*)

■ a sense of finality (*And that was the last time I ever saw my best friend.*).

Endings should fit the mood of the story and what has gone before, and provide a conclusion of some kind. You don't want to sound as if you simply ran out of ink, time, space or ideas. A sudden change of mood or character behaviour would not sound convincing. You should know your ending before you start writing so that you can work towards it, without spoiling the suspense by giving it away. The title may hint at the kind of story it is but should not reveal how it will end.

16 Below are seven narrative titles with which to practise your planning skills. Choose three of them, and give yourself five minutes on each to develop a plan for a story.

    a 'I had to think quickly if I was to stay out of trouble.'

    b The box

    c No regrets

    d The chance of a lifetime

    e The letter which arrived too late

    f Look before you leap

    g 'A thing of beauty is a joy for ever.' Write a story inspired by this line of poetry.

17 Choose one of your plans from Activity **16** to turn into a mini-saga (a complete narrative consisting of exactly 50 words). You will need to draft and edit until you get the length exactly right, considering which content is essential and how the use of syntax and sentence structure affects the word count (e.g. hyphenated words and participle phrases reduce it, simple sentences and passive forms increase it). Read your mini-saga to the rest of the class, who will vote on a winner.

TASK TIP

Narrative question titles can take different forms (e.g. short phrase, quotation, proverb, continuation of an opening sentence, using the given final sentence). Bear in mind that there are different kinds of narrative (e.g. science fiction, comedy, detective), and there is no reason why you should not write an exam composition or coursework piece in any genre, provided that you are familiar with its features and can make it engaging for the reader.

When planning a story, it is usually better not to attempt to reproduce a piece of writing you have done before, as it is likely to sound stale and incoherent, and may not be fully relevant to the set title. Make sure that your plan pays attention to the opening and ending, and contains at least six paragraph headings (and so would develop into at least 400 words). Indicate the time frame of the narrative, where dialogue and description will be included and where the story's climax will occur.

89

18 Read the following complete short story aloud as a class, sharing the narrative parts and with two students playing the role of the narrator and the girl in the dialogues.

The eyes have it

I had the train compartment to myself up to Rohana, then a girl got in. The couple who saw her off were probably her parents; they seemed very anxious about her comfort, and the woman gave the girl detailed instructions as to where to keep her things, when not to lean out of windows, and how to avoid speaking to strangers.

They called their goodbyes and the train pulled out of the station. As I was totally blind at the time, my eyes sensitive only to light and darkness, I was unable to tell what the girl looked like; but I knew she wore slippers from the way they slapped against her heels.

It would take me some time to discover something about her looks, and perhaps I never would. But I liked the sound of her voice, and even the sound of her slippers.

'Are you going all the way to Dehra?' I asked.

I must have been sitting in a dark corner, because my voice startled her. She gave a little exclamation and said, 'I didn't know anyone else was here.'

Well, it often happens that people with good eyesight fail to see what is right in front of them. They have too much to take in, I suppose. Whereas people who cannot see (or see very little) have to take in only the essentials, whatever registers most tellingly on their remaining senses.

'I didn't see you either,' I said. 'But I heard you come in.'

I wondered if I would be able to prevent her from discovering that I was blind. Provided I keep to my seat, I thought, it shouldn't be too difficult.

The girl said, 'I'm getting off at Saharanpur. My aunt is meeting me there.'

'Then I had better not get too familiar,' I replied. 'Aunts are usually formidable creatures.'

'Where are you going?' she asked.

'To Dehra, and then to Mussoorie.'

'Oh, how lucky you are. I wish I were going to Mussoorie. I love the hills. Especially in October.'

'Yes, this is the best time,' I said, calling on my memories. 'The hills are covered with wild dahlias, the sun is delicious, and at night you can sit in front of a logfire and drink a little brandy. Most of the tourists have gone, and the roads are quiet and almost deserted. Yes, October is the best time.'

She was silent. I wondered if my words had touched her, or whether she thought me a romantic fool. Then I made a mistake.

'What is it like outside?' I asked.

She seemed to find nothing strange in the question. Had she noticed already that I could not see? But her next question removed my doubts.

'Why don't you look out of the window?' she asked.

I moved easily along the berth and felt for the window ledge. The window was open, and I faced it, making a pretence of studying the landscape. I heard the panting of the engine, the rumble of the wheels, and, in my mind's eye, I could see telegraph posts flashing by.

'Have you noticed,' I ventured, 'that the trees seem to be moving while we seem to be standing still?'

'That always happens,' she said. 'Do you see any animals?'

'No,' I answered quite confidently. I knew that there were hardly any animals left in the forests near Dehra.

I turned from the window and faced the girl, and for a while we sat in silence.

'You have an interesting face,' I remarked. I was becoming quite daring, but it was a safe remark. Few girls can resist flattery. She laughed pleasantly – a clear, ringing laugh.

'It's nice to be told I have an interesting face. I'm tired of people telling me I have a pretty face.'

Oh, so you do have a pretty face, thought I: and aloud I said: 'Well, an interesting face can also be pretty.'

'You are a very gallant young man,' she said, 'but why are you so serious?'

I thought, then, I would try to laugh for her, but the thought of laughter only made me feel troubled and lonely.

'We'll soon be at your station,' I said.

'Thank goodness it's a short journey. I can't bear to sit in a train for more than two-or-three hours.'

Yet I was prepared to sit there for almost any length of time, just to listen to her talking. Her voice had the

sparkle of a mountain stream. As soon as she left the train, she would forget our brief encounter; but it would stay with me for the rest of the journey, and for some time after.

The engine's whistle shrieked, the carriage wheels changed their sound and rhythm, the girl got up and began to collect her things. I wondered if she wore her hair in bun, or if it was plaited; perhaps it was hanging loose over her shoulders, or was it cut very short?

The train drew slowly into the station. Outside, there was the shouting of porters and vendors and a high-pitched female voice near the carriage door; that voice must have belonged to the girl's aunt.

'Goodbye,' the girl said.

She was standing very close to me, so close that the perfume from her hair was tantalizing. I wanted to raise my hand and touch her hair, but she moved away. Only the scent of perfume still lingered where she had stood.

There was some confusion in the doorway. A man, getting into the compartment, stammered an apology. Then the door banged, and the world was shut out again. I returned to my berth. The guard blew his whistle and we moved off. Once again, I had a game to play and a new fellow-traveller.

The train gathered speed, the wheels took up their song, the carriage groaned and shook. I found the window and sat in front of it, staring into the daylight that was darkness for me.

So many things were happening outside the window: it could be a fascinating game, guessing what went on out there.

The man who had entered the compartment broke into my reverie.

'You must be disappointed,' he said. 'I'm not nearly as attractive a travelling companion as the one who just left.'

'She was an interesting girl,' I said. 'Can you tell me – did she keep her hair long or short?'

'I don't remember,' he said, sounding puzzled. 'It was her eyes I noticed, not her hair. She had beautiful eyes – but they were of no use to her. She was completely blind. Didn't you notice?'

Short story by Ruskin Bond.

19 Work in small groups to prepare comments on the following aspects of the short story in Activity **18**:

   a the plot and its ironies

   b the setting and structure

   c the use of dialogue

   d the first and last sentences

   e the title.

20 In your groups, imagine that you are examiners who want to use this story as the passage in a reading exam paper.

   How would you reduce it to no more than 750 words? (It is currently 1095 words). Put brackets around parts you think could be removed without spoiling the story. Discuss what difference your cuts have made to the overall effect. Your teacher will monitor your discussion.

21 **a** Give the story a new title.

   b Write your own new ending to the story, as an extra paragraph to the story. What kind of ending would be appropriate? (Remind yourself of the list in the Task tip below Activity **15**). Read your new ending to the class, who will vote on the best.

➕ Further practice

   a Complete the story you started in Activity **12**. This could be for a coursework assignment if it is between length guidelines.

   b Select your best plan from Activity **16** and develop it into a narrative composition of 350–450 words.

   c Read the small ads below, which come from a magazine, and choose one on which to base a plan for a narrative to explain it.

WANTED: empty jam jars and bottles.

Urgent!

Danni, come home, it was all a mistake. Love mum.

FREE alpaca wool available in large quantities.

Phone this number ...

Part 4:
Ideas and technology

Unit 10: Reading Comprehension

This unit continues to develop summary skills, collation of material, recognition of implicit meanings and attitudes, and identification of language effects. It also gives practice in vocabulary building and advanced punctuation.

1 Read the following informative article from a hobbies magazine.

2 Select a list of topic phrases from the passage. Compare your list with a partner's.

3 What are the opinions of the writer of this article on the subject of photography? Give quotations to support your answer.

4 Scan the text then complete the following statements. Remember to reduce the number of words and to change them into your own.

 a The invention of photography changed the world because …

 b The best photographs are those which …

 c Artistry is the ability to …

 d A skilful photographer will …

 e Experience is important because …

The art and science of photography

When photography was first invented it changed the world: what people saw could be recorded as it really was without the intervention of an artist. Photography as historical record has been very important ever since. But equally important, the very first pioneers saw that it, too, was an art form, not merely a way of documenting reality. True photographers are artists of the camera.

Photography is enthralling because it is both an art and a science. It is an art over which the photographer has creative control but only to a certain extent: unlike a painter, you can only take photographs of what is there. If the sun is not shining, you cannot photograph sunlight. So you need to find a subject. But the greatest photographs are of subjects that most people would have walked past without noticing. The truly great photographers are those who can see, in their mind's eye, the photograph that they can create through their vision, artistry and skill.

Vision comes first. If you cannot see the potential, you can never be a true photographer. Artistry, by contrast, can be learned and developed; you can read a book or you take lessons. You can learn from a great practitioner. Perhaps the simplest aspect to describe is framing.

The human eye has a huge field of view, stretching almost 180 degrees. The lens of a camera, by contrast, has a very restricted field of view. This is both a curse and a blessing. Try as you might, you cannot capture the sheer scale of the human perspective of the world. But you can, and must, select the image that you are attempting to capture – or rather, to create. Look through the viewfinder: learn to see the world through the lens. Understand the difference it makes when you remove the irrelevant and select only what really matters. That is artistry.

Next comes skill. This is the technical part. Skill is exercised long before you even start to look for a subject: there are a series of essential decisions which you have to take. Do you want to use a traditional roll-film camera, or a digital one? Each of them has advantages – and drawbacks. Now that all cameras are in effect mini-computers, there is a temptation to leave much of the decision-making to the electronics inside, but the true photographer will override the factory settings to retain control over the details of exposure, focus and contrast. Once the photograph is taken, great skill is required to produce the final article, whether through the processing and printing of roll-film, or by digital manipulation using image-adjustment software on a computer.

Experience teaches you about all of these; there is no other way to learn than to try, possibly to fail, but to learn from the experience and improve. This is what marks out the photographer from those who merely take snapshots. There is always a better photograph that could have been taken – the ultimate photograph, if you like. All photographers pursue this goal of perfection. In the process, though, they take some beautiful photographs which bring them joy thereafter.

Of course, this is art photography. To most people most of the time, 'photography' is making an instant recording of a moment. Now that virtually all mobile phones have built-in cameras – many, now, with professional-quality resolution – everybody has become a 'photographer' in the sense that they can capture an instant, without preparation or thought or having to remember to take a 'camera'. The world's news media rely increasingly on ordinary people who just happened to be there when some news event occurred, and snapped or video-recorded it, then instantly uploaded the images via a mobile-phone network.

In this sense, 'photography' has changed the world again. And, through social media, there is now an obsession with capturing, and displaying for all the world to see, images – zany, manipulated, unreal much of the time – on Facebook or Instagram. Whether this is 'art', or indeed of any value at all, I leave my audience to judge.

5 Read the following magazine article, which describes how a Russian built and sailed his own submarine.

One man and his sub

Even in the often **surreal** world of inventions, Mikhail Puchkov's creation has to rank as one of the more **bizarre**: a pedal-powered one-man mini submarine.

Actually, he no longer needs the pedals, although they are still there at the front of his steel craft. 'I used to pedal for electricity, but that was too exhausting,' he says. So some time ago Puchkov installed a car battery and lengthened the craft to its present 5 m. This scarcely qualifies as a **conventional** vessel. Surrounded by the masts of St Petersburg's Nautical Institute Yacht Club, where Puchkov is based in summer, the do-it-yourself submarine looks particularly out of place.

Sipping tea and smoking cigarettes in front of the club's rusty metal huts, Puchkov explains the basics of his invention. When he is on the surface he relies on an ordinary, if noisy, petrol-powered motorbike engine – starting it up sounds like someone drilling through a wall – and navigates by global positioning satellites. Underwater, he switches to an electric motor (now powered by the battery) and old-fashioned compasses and maps for navigation (there is no periscope). Oxygen is supplied from a bottle 'filled with normal air'. The sub goes to a maximum depth of 10 m and reaches a top speed of 8 km an hour, which, he observes, is '3 km per hour faster than the average person walks'. This eccentric device, shaped rather like a helicopter (Puchkov actually

tried to build a helicopter before he **embarked on** this scheme), is all the more remarkable for having been built in total secrecy at the height of the Soviet **regime**. When he left the army in 1981, Puchkov, now 40, spent six years **painstakingly** putting it together in his spare time while he worked in a factory in Ryazan, his home town, south-east of Moscow.

He is **evasive** about where the money came from, though some of the materials he was able to **elicit** from contacts in the local steel mill. Even his closest friends and family did not know of the existence of the sub, which was kept under a specially constructed cover.

When he was ready, in 1987, he set out along the river Tosna, near Moscow, and managed to sail hundreds of miles as far as the river Neva, which flows through St Petersburg – or Leningrad as it was then known. He was guiding the sub northwards towards the open waters of the Gulf of Finland when it became trapped in a logjam of wood. There was no way to escape, so he was forced to come to the surface; his long-kept secret was out in the open.

'The KGB arrived to arrest me,' Puchkov says. 'They searched the whole submarine for photographs and sent ships to the Gulf of Finland to look for my "accomplices".' The secret service held him in **custody** for a week; <u>family and friends back home were grilled</u>. 'After a while

they worked out that it was all a joke and that I didn't intend to use my sub to spy on anyone.' Then, in <u>an extraordinary volte-face</u>, the authorities sent him to study at a nautical institute in Leningrad. As a result he was offered a job in the navy – which he **declined**.

Today Puchkov spends October to May working in a glass factory and living in a shared flat. On sunny days he likes to sail to the uninhabited islands in the Gulf of Finland. It isn't all <u>plain sailing</u>: in heavy seas, when the ventilator cannot cope, the overpowering smell of petrol fumes in the cabin makes Puchkov seasick.

But taking risks is part of the thrill for a **dare-devil**. 'The further out you go, the more frightening it becomes,' he smiles **sheepishly**. 'There is always the possibility that you won't come back.'

Adapted from an article by Nicholas Brautlecht, *The Sunday Times*, 2001.

Mini-sub statistics

Length 5 m

Width 1 m

Operating depth 10 m (max)

Height 1.2 m

Speed 8 kph (max)

Weight 1.8 tonnes

Range 300–400 km

6 a **Twelve** words or phrases are in bold in the article about the submarine. Replace them with synonyms which fit the context. Notice that many of them are figurative or have a particular meaning in this context. Use a dictionary for any you do not know, and add any new words to your personal vocabulary list.

   b The following phrases are underlined in the article. Explain them in your own words:

   ■ family and friends back home were grilled

   ■ an extraordinary volte-face

   ■ plain sailing.

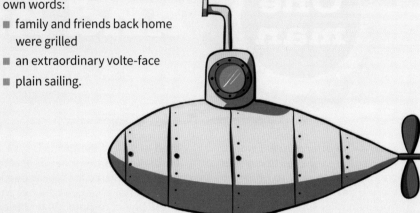

7 Discuss in class whether the headlines below would make good alternative headlines to the article. For each, say why or why not. Can you think of an even better one?

Mikhail's mad invention

Do-it-yourself submarine

Pedal power!

KGB ARREST SPY SUSPECT

Seasick sailor's secret

8   Quote a range of words/phrases from the article that show that the writer:

   a   thinks Puchkov's achievement is strange but impressive

   b   does not admire the Soviets or the KGB.

9   Find the hyphens, dashes, brackets, colons and semicolons in the article about the submarine. After discussion with your partner, complete the following sentences to explain the differences between them.

   a   Hyphens, which link two or three words without spaces in between, are used to ... .

   b   They are also used at the end of a line of writing to show that a word ... .

   c   Dashes, which are twice the width of hyphens and which have spaces before and after them, are used either singly to ... or as a pair to ... .

   d   Brackets are always used in pairs, and they show that ... .

   e   Colons indicate that ... .

   f   Semicolons perform the role of ... .

10   Using the facts in the 'Mini-sub statistics' box and from the article, write three sentences to describe the submarine's appearance and performance, focusing on these characteristics:

   a   its dimensions

   b   its movement

   c   its power.

11   Select the facts which give information about Puchkov himself. Write a paragraph of about 100 words which:

   a   gives his life story

   b   describes his character.

12   Check your piece of writing is the right length, legible, comprehensive, and accurate in content and expression.

   Your partner will mark your summary out of 20 (15 for reading, 5 for writing) and write a comment on it. A top reading mark means that all the relevant information has been used, with no irrelevant material included; a top writing mark means that the summary is expressed clearly and concisely, mainly in your own words.

13 Read the magazine advertisement below.

Keep your dishes sparkling the easy way, say the experts.
Make sure that your dishwasher is squeaky clean –
by using Crystal Clear Dishwasher Cleaner.

The solution is Crystal Clear

The dishwasher is one of the greatest inventions of all time: when you've had a busy day, it's such a relief to know that you can put your whole family's used plates, bowls, glasses, mugs and cutlery in the machine and let it do all the work for you. But are you looking after your dishwasher as well as it looks after you? Over time, grease and limescale can accumulate inside your machine and start causing problems, and if you don't take action, those problems will only get worse. The solution is actually very simple: you use *Crystal Clear Dishwasher Cleaner* to make everything fresh and sparkling again.

The interior of your dishwasher may look clean, but grime can easily build up in unseen and hard-to-reach areas – in the pipes, on the spray arms, in the filter and the heating element. When that happens, you will notice that your machine isn't cleaning dishes as well as it normally does – there may be food residues or water marks, your plates might be wet, and your glasses may start looking cloudy. Bad odours are another tell-tale sign that it's time for a good clean. You and your family will notice the difference immediately – because a thoroughly clean dishwasher means thoroughly clean and shining dishes.

Research has shown that a shocking 15 kg of grease and limescale passes through a dishwasher during its lifetime, and 54% of consumers have reported noticing unpleasant odours in their machines.

But you can say goodbye to bad smells and blockages as well as unsatisfactory results with *Crystal Clear Dishwasher Cleaner.*

14 Plan and write an analysis of the advertisement in about 300 words, commenting on the following aspects:
- suppositions the writer has made about the audience
- vocabulary which you think is effective, and why
- the range of emotions evoked and how the writer achieves this
- persuasive devices
- the combined effect of the language and the images used.

15 Read the passage below describing the Inca site of Machu Picchu.

Machu Picchu is a 15th-century Inca site located 2430 m above sea level in Peru. It is situated on a mountain ridge above the Sacred Valley, which is 80 km northwest of Cusco, the Inca capital, and through which the Urubamba River flows. Most archaeologists believe that Machu Picchu was built as an estate for the Inca emperor Pachacuti (1438–72). Often referred to as the 'Lost City of the Incas', it is perhaps the most familiar **icon** of Inca civilisation. It is one of the most important archaeological sites in all of Latin America, and the most visited tourist attraction in Peru.

It is generally believed to be a sacred religious site, but a **plethora** of other theories have been proposed. One maintains that Machu Picchu was an Inca *llaqta*, a settlement built to control the economy of **conquered** regions. Another asserts that it may have been built as a prison for a select few who had committed **heinous** crimes against Inca society. Yet another hypothesis is that it is an agricultural testing station, because of the high location and the terraces. Other theories suggests that the city was built as an **abode** for the **deities**,

99

or for the coronation of kings. It was built in the classical Inca style, with polished dry-stone walls. Its three primary structures are the *Intihuatana* (Hitching Post of the Sun), the Temple of the Sun, and the Room of the Three Windows. These are located in what is known by archaeologists as the Sacred District of Machu Picchu.

The Incas built the estate around 1450, at the height of the Inca empire, but abandoned it a century later at the time of the Spanish Conquest. Although the citadel is located only about 80 km from Cusco, the Spanish never found it and **consequently** did not **plunder** or destroy it, as they did many other sites. Over the centuries, the surrounding jungle grew over much of the site, and few outsiders knew of its existence before it was brought to international attention in 1911 by the American historian Hiram Bingham. Since then, Machu Picchu has become an important tourist attraction. Most of the outlying buildings have been reconstructed in order to give tourists a better idea of what they originally looked like. By 1976, 30% of Machu Picchu had been restored. The restoration work continues to this day. It was declared a Peruvian Historical Sanctuary in 1981 and a UNESCO World Heritage Site in 1983. In 2007, Machu Picchu was voted one of the New Seven Wonders of the World in a worldwide internet poll.

Machu Picchu is vulnerable to threats from a variety of sources. While natural **phenomena** like earthquakes and weather systems can interfere with access, the site also suffers from the pressures of too many tourists. In addition, preservation of the area's cultural and archaeological heritage is an ongoing concern.

TASK TIP

Non-fiction informative texts (such as those about historical or scientific topics) are written in the formal and impersonal style appropriate for textbooks. You can expect to find passive verbs, complex and varied sentences, technical/sophisticated vocabulary and many statistics and names, all of which contribute to the impression that the writer is a mature, knowledgeable, articulate, trustworthy authority on the subject and that the information is purely factual and unbiased.

16 Work with a partner. Replace the **nine** words in bold in the passage with words or phrases of your own which mean exactly the same and which do not occur in the passage.

17 Various verbs used in informative articles can be approximately synonymous but have different strengths of meaning. As a class, rank the words below in order of strength, using 1 for the weakest:

■ claim ■ maintain ■ assert ■ say ■ state ■ opine ■ observe ■ mention ■ declare ■ suggest

18 Explain in a paragraph, with examples of vocabulary and syntax, how the style of the passage conveys its genre, purpose and effect.

19 Read the following passage about Inca architecture.

THE AMAZING INCAS

Incas, like the ancient Egyptians, had occult knowledge through which they wrought miracles of engineering. Their cities, their roads, their stonemasonry are astonishing – the Inca jigsaw foundations have withstood everything that nature can throw at them. They still stand, an art form in their own right, as silent tributes to the skills of unknown stonemasons, to the unique survival of the Incas.

The Incas never used the wheel in any practical manner. How they moved and placed the enormous blocks of stones remains an enigma, although the general belief is that they used hundreds of men to push the stones up inclined planes. Peru is an earthquake region so they cleverly used special features to prevent destruction: the trapezoidal shape of doors and windows provided greater stability, and without mortar, dry-stone walls can move and re-settle without collapsing. The Incas were masters of this technique, called ashlar, in which blocks of stone are cut to fit together so perfectly that it is said not even a blade of grass fits between them.

The location of the city was a military secret, and its deep precipices and steep mountains provided excellent natural defences. It could be accessed only by bridges across the surrounding river gorge, and these, made of rope or horizontal tree trunks, could be removed if the city was threatened by invaders. It has a water supply from springs that cannot be blocked easily, and enough land to grow food for about four times as many people as ever lived there. The hillsides leading to it have been terraced, not only to provide more farmland to grow crops, but to steepen the slopes which invaders would have to ascend. The terraces reduced soil erosion and protected against landslides. Regardless of its original purpose, it is strategically located and readily defended.

The Peruvians claim the magnificent site of Machu Picchu as the eighth wonder of the world. But Machu Picchu is overrun by tourists. It is in danger of becoming a modern theme park. The manicured lawns provide a battery recharge for exhausted backpackers who have just completed the Inca Trail. Gardeners work continually on restoring walls and cultivating the terraces. Present-day Peru displays all the problems of a growing country. The modern myth is that history, perhaps, holds the key to their solution.

TASK TIP

The passage in Activity **19** has an obvious viewpoint and bias, which is admiration for the Incas and their architectural achievements. This makes the passage less strictly informative and more personal and **discursive** than the first one. This also shows in the style: use of idioms, figurative language, emotive vocabulary, non-technical vocabulary, speculative adverbs and informal sentence structures. The passages are of the types that are used in many exam reading papers.

20 Explain the following phrases in your own words.

    a *had occult knowledge through which they wrought miracles*

    b *remains an enigma*

    c *reduced soil erosion*

    d *it is strategically located and readily defended*

    e *The manicured lawns provide a battery recharge*

21 Draw a grid like the one below and then complete it with a partner to compare the two texts in Activities **15** and **19**.

	Text 1	Text 1
content		
vocabulary		
syntax and sentence type		
purpose and audience		
overall effect		

22 Read this travel writing extract about a planned visit to Machu Picchu.

IN SEARCH OF THE LOST CITY

I was surprised by the size of the figure that appeared around the street corner. I had heard that Eduard was a Ukrainian who had fled from home many years ago. They say Ukrainians are often well-built, but Eduard was more than that: he was a great bear of a man; and to complete the picture, he was wearing a bearskin coat. But, to be fair, he needed it for his job as a guide, high up in the Andes, where it is bitterly cold.

'Hi Madiha!' he called. Fortunately, he spoke good English (the only language we had in common), as I know neither Spanish nor Russian and he had no French or Arabic. 'Fancy a coffee?'

My journey to Peru from my home country of Egypt had been a long and indirect one, literally and metaphorically. I had started with an academic interest in geologic history, particularly the prehistoric changes to the world's land masses that took place millions of years ago. I was fascinated by the idea that South America was once joined with Africa, Australia and Antarctica in a huge land mass, which scientists have named Gondwanaland. Many years after the continents separated and drifted apart, it is thought that humans crossed the Bering Strait land bridge from Asia, and moved down through North America and into Central and South America. My recent obsession was with the civilization of the Incas, who settled in the Peruvian mountains and made amazing scientific and technological achievements. Now I planned to 'follow the Inca trail' to see the sites for myself. Of all the wonders these people had achieved, none surpassed the magnificence of the long-lost mountain refuge of Machu Picchu: a miracle of town planning erected at the summit of the impenetrable Andes.

Eduard the Bear settled into a chair in the cafe – or rather, he spread out over it.

'How can I help you, Madiha?'

'I want to see the real Machu Picchu.'

Eduard laughed mirthlessly. 'So which one would that be? The one that the pilgrim-visitors used to seek, trekking for days up the mountains, carrying their supplies and tents on their backs? Or the one the spoilt, rich kids want to drop in on, preferably by helicopter, without having to make any effort at all?' He paused. 'You can't move in the city any more for all the package tourists. They gain no understanding of the place; just tick it off their list. You only get out what you put in!' Another pause. 'The breath-taking first view as you emerge at the top of the trail after days of back-breaking toil – that's how Machu Picchu should be seen.'

I smiled. 'Well, I don't intend to use a helicopter. Haven't they been banned anyway?'

Eduard nodded. 'The Peruvian authorities are torn: they like the money from the tourists, but they hate the damage they do. They're trying to limit invasive visits, get back to the simple, old ways …'

This gave me my opening. 'Actually, I'd like to see it the way Bingham first saw it in 1911.'

Now it was Eduard's turn to smile. I admired Hiram Bingham, and I wanted to walk in his steps and share the wonder he must have felt as he gazed on the ruins of Machu Picchu – the first visitor for 300 years. As an American academic at Yale, he had heard the legend that, at the time of the Spanish Conquistadors, the Incas had created a final refuge 'in the clouds' to which they could escape with their most precious cultural artefacts. No one had really believed in this place any more than in the equally lost golden city of El Dorado, which generations of explorers had sought in vain. But Bingham actually found his lost city – and now I wanted to find it too.

23 Say, in your own words, what you have learned from the passage about:

   a the narrator
   b the guide
   c Hiram Bingham
   d the people who used to visit Machu Picchu
   e the people who now visit Machu Picchu.

24 With a partner, make notes on the passage to prepare for a class discussion on the features of travel writing. Think about:

- use of character
- use of dialogue
- type of vocabulary
- sentence structures
- voice and viewpoint
- content.

➕ Further practice

a   Write notes, in your own words, taken from the boxed text below, for each of the following summary titles:

- Human attitudes to wolves
- Why wolves are beneficial to the environment
- How the relationship with wolves can be improved

Wolves have been persecuted for centuries. Human attitudes will determine whether our top predators can survive in Europe in the 21st century. Most Europeans have lost the traditional knowledge of how to cope with large carnivores and of how humans and predators can coexist. Local people can actually benefit from working with carnivores. By promoting eco-tourism, a country's tourist industry can be extended. Understandably, there is concern about livestock casualties, but throughout history shepherds have effectively used traditional guarding methods with dogs, and sheep and cattle have been protected by being put in pens at night. Public awareness is needed to counteract the view of wolves as wicked, cunning and merciless. This negative image is fuelled by popular mythology and children's stories, and is based on fear rather than fact. Wolves are actually social, timid animals that avoid contact with humans. Wolf attacks on people are extremely rare, but shedding their bloodthirsty reputation involves public education on many levels. These include educational visits, publicity in the international media and the distribution of literature.

b Plan and write an **editorial** on a science or technology topic currently in national or international news, for example robots, space travel, medical treatment, wind farms. Summarise the situation and then argue for or against it being a welcome development. Write about 300 words. Give it a headline.

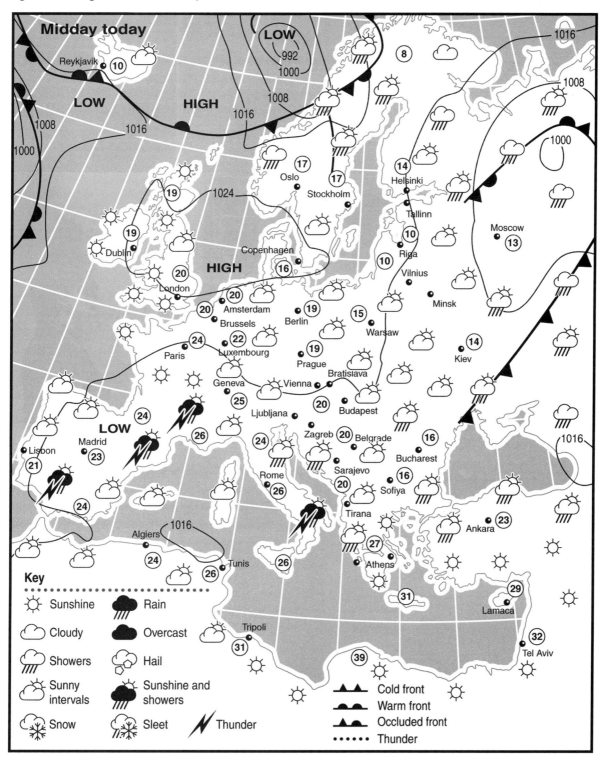

b Study the meteorological chart above. Analyse and organise the data in it. Write a weather-forecast script for television or radio, of about 300 words. Express yourself clearly and precisely, and try to avoid repeating vocabulary and grammatical structures.

Unit 11: Response Writing

This unit gives practice in selecting suitable content, structure and style for argumentative and discursive responses to texts. It also gives advice on spelling strategies, pairs of punctuation marks and rhetorical devices.

1   Should you believe everything you read in the newspapers? Is news reporting always purely informative? Discuss this topic as a class. Notice which students sound more convincing when they express their views. Why do you think this is?

2   Read the three news reports which follow. (Note: the spelling is American.)

Text A

LAKEWOOD TOWNSHIP, N.J. (CBS NewYork) – Police in Lakewood Township, N.J., were on alert Monday after a fox attacked a child.

The fox reportedly scratched a 4-year-old girl on her arm, leg and lip this past Saturday near Ocean Avenue in Lakewood Township, authorities said.

Animal control officers found the fox and killed it. But people who lived nearby were still concerned Monday.

'Growing up here, you've seen squirrels and cats, but I've certainly never seen any foxes,' one man said.

Animal control officials said results of a rabies test on the animal should be out on Tuesday.

Adapted from http://worldnewsviews.com/2013/07/29/lakewood-township-n-j-residents-concerned-after-fox-attack/

Text B

FOX ATTACKS TODDLER IN LAKEWOOD

Lakewood police shot and killed a fox after the animal bit a three-year-old girl walking with a sibling on 14th Street on Saturday night.

When cops arrived, the fox was hanging out under a neighbor's deck and attacked them, prompting police to shoot and kill it, according to the Lakewood Scoop. The child was taken to Kimball Medical Center in Lakewood to be treated for scratches to her arm leg and lip.

'Police Officer Matt Moore found the fox under the resident's deck and was forced to fire his duty weapon at the fox after it tried to attack him and a Lakewood Animal Control officer,' Lakewood Police Lieutenant Steve Allaire tells the Lakewood Scoop.

The fox is being tested for rabies. Lakewood Police Lieutenant Steve Allaire tells TLS, 'Injuries could have been worse to the victim, but during the initial attack an unidentified male ran over and was able to kick the fox away from the child.'

Adapted from http://wobm.com/fox-attacks-toddler-in-lakewood/
and http://wobm.com/author/dianned13/

Text C

Fox that attacked little girl in New Jersey tested positive for rabies

Tuesday, July 30, 2013, Nina Pineda & Jennifer Matarese, Eyewitness News

LAKEWOOD, N.J. (WABC) – A fox that attacked a four-year-old girl in Lakewood, New Jersey has tested positive for rabies.

She will receive a rabies-prevention treatment for 14 days and officials will closely monitor her condition.

'I heard screaming,' said Eli Abad, a neighbor.

Eli Abad showed Eyewitness News with his hands how big the wild animal was that terrorized his young neighbor on Saturday.

It was a blondish red fox, one common in the area.

The child had been playing in her backyard with her mother she told the Lakewood Police the fox came out of nowhere, scratching her daughter arms and legs with its sharp claws hard enough to draw blood.

Animal control was also on the scene according to Lt. Steve Allaire.

He was unauthorized to speak on camera but told Eyewitness News they were attempting to put a snare around the fox's head when it became vicious and a police officer fired twice to put the animal down.

The fox died at the scene.

Sightings like this are rare though and foxes aren't known to attack.

Kids were inside or behind fences in the neighborhood and many parents said they'll be extremely careful while their children play outside.

Adapted from http://abclocal.go.com/wabc/story?section=news/local/new_jersey&id=9188499

TASK TIP

Unlike a news report, whose aim should be informative, a newspaper, magazine or blog article comments on a topical issue or recent event and is discursive or argumentative. It can use the first person, which a news report never does.

Paragraphs, though still short by comparison with other kinds of writing, are longer in an article than in a report, and the facts are expressed in a less condensed way. For example, in a news report you might say: *36-year-old former schoolteacher and mother of two, Sadaf Kassim, says ...*, whereas in an article it might be: *Sadaf Kassim, who is in her mid-thirties, has two children, and used to be a teacher in a junior school, believes that ...*

3 Make preparatory notes and then feed back to the class the effects of the following in Texts A, B and C:

   a the different content

   b the different style

   c the different headline.

4 Decide with a partner and indicate on a copy of the passages the facts and the opinions contained in each report.

5 Agree with your partner on answers to the following questions about the reports:

   a Which contains most facts?

   b Which contains most opinions?

   c Which one did you find most informative?

   d Which one did you find most emotive?

6 Plan and write a blog article of 250–350 words in which you:

   a express your own reaction to the fox attack news story, referring to the content of the three versions, collating and ordering the facts in your own words and without repetition.

   b give your views on news reporting generally, using ideas from the discussion in Activity **1**.

   Give your article a suitable title.

7 Read the newspaper article below on the subject of luck.

Scientist believes that we make our own luck

Born lucky? Probably not. Scientists undertaking the biggest study yet into the role luck plays in people's lives say that we are almost certainly the masters of our own destinies.

Researchers from the Institute of Child Health at Bristol University have begun a study of 14,000 children to try to discover whether we are ruled by fate or can create our own luck.

Over the next two years the children will be asked a series of questions about self-esteem, achievement and the role of luck. Researchers will use this to try to ascertain why some people – and we all know some – always seem to land on their feet.

'Some people cope with all sorts of adversities and we want to find out why,' said Professor Jean Goulding, the project director.

Steve Nowicki, a clinical psychologist and visiting professor at Emory University, Atlanta, who will play a key role in the study, has been working on the subject for 30 years and believes he already knows the answer. His work suggests that luck is a triumph of nurture over nature and that people's personalities influence how they are treated by fate.

He believes that, when confronted by a problem, people fall into two groups: internalists and externalists. 'Internalists analyse, act and learn from whatever the outcome is. Externalists believe they have no control over their fate and they are passive. If they fall over, they just blame bad fortune instead of trying to work out why and how to prevent it happening again.'

The willingness of externalists to see the hand of fate in what has happened makes them liable to more 'bad luck'. Nowicki's research suggests they are more likely to drift into a life of crime than internalists, who tend to become high achievers.

Which group a child grows into depends most importantly on the influence of parents, grandparents, teachers and peers. Nowicki suggests children from rich backgrounds are more likely to become externalists than children from poor backgrounds, who have had to overcome adversity to succeed. A rare argument for the advantages of poverty!

Adapted from *The Sunday Times*, 2001.

8 Express the following phrases from the article in your own words. You may need to refer to a dictionary. Compare your answers with your partner's and decide which is better in each case.

   a *the masters of our own destinies*

   b *to land on their feet*

   c *all sorts of adversities*

   d *triumph of nurture over nature*

   e *drift into a life of crime*

KEY POINT

A discursive response looks at a topic from various points of view and does not take sides; the aim is to inform. Argument, on the other hand, adopts a definite position and presents a case for it being the only correct view; it takes account of the alternative case only to demolish it, as the aim is to persuade.

Your own personal view is the one you are likely to argue most convincingly. However, you may be asked to respond on a subject you have not considered before, or about which you have no particular view, and you will still need to write convincingly, which means being able to provide support for the points you make.

The skill of engaging with a text and responding discursively or argumentatively is required for some exam writing tasks and coursework assignments.

9 a Discuss in class how you feel about luck and whether you think you are a lucky person or not. Find out what the majority of the class believe on this subject. Note which students sound more persuasive, and why.

b Plan and write an argumentative response to the article in the form of a letter to Steve Nowicki, in which you express your own views on his opinions and research. Give examples from your own experience and from the class discussion in **a**.

10 The words listed below are useful in argument and discussion. They are also difficult to spell.

acknowledge	excellent	phenomenon
acquaintance	existence	possession
appropriate	experience	prejudice
attempt	extremely	privilege
beautiful	foreign	psychological
beginning	government	pursue
business	immediately	receive
campaign	independent	reminiscent
completely	interesting	responsibility
conscience	irrelevant	separate
criticism	liaison	skilful
decision	miniature	specific
definitely	necessary	subtle
disappearance	noticeable	successful
embarrassment	occasionally	surprise
enthusiasm	occurred	temporary
environment	opportunity	thorough
especially	parliament	unique
exaggerate	miniscule	vulnerable

a Look at the words and discuss with your partner why each of them is difficult to spell. Identify the 'hot spot' in each word (i.e. the precise point of difficulty).

b Are there any words whose spelling surprises you, that you have misspelt in the past or that you regularly get wrong? Make a list.

c Focus for five seconds on the hot spot in each word in your list.

d Test yourself on these words, using the Look–Cover–Write–Check method, which means covering the word while you write it from memory and then comparing your answer with the correct spelling.

e Learn any words you got wrong by continuing to focus on the hot spot of the correct spelling and retesting until you get them right

TASK TIP

Although you are unlikely to be penalised in an exam for misspelling an individual word, mechanical accuracy is obviously important in an English language examination. It shows a lack of care and attention to misspell a word that exists in the text. Sometimes spelling errors can create confusion and you cannot expect to do well in a writing paper if your spelling is consistently weak. You can improve your spelling by using these strategies:

- Always correct spelling errors in returned work. (It's the only way to learn them.)
- Never guess a spelling. (This reinforces errors.)
- Don't rely on a computer spellcheck. (It can be misleading.)
- Take into account the prefix if the word has one. (e.g. *ob(p) - pression, dis-satisfaction*).
- Notice which letter strings are possible in English (e.g. *qu* but never *qi; -tion* but not *-toin* for nouns, *'ely'* but not *'ley'* for adverbs).
- Compare with words with the same linguistic derivation in other languages, such as French, Italian or Spanish (e.g. bureaucracy, naive, anniversary).
- Use the Look–Cover–Write–Check method (which plants a visual image of the whole word in your mind.)
- Make up **mnemonics**, acronyms and rhymes to help you (e.g. *It is necessary for one coat to have two sleeves*, i.e. there is a single *c* and a double *s* in necessary).
- Group words with silent letters (e.g. *debt/doubt; knot/knob*).
- Find words in other words (e.g. *science* in *conscience; finite* in *definitely*).
- With difficult long words, separate the syllables in your mind (e.g. *Wed-nes-day, extra-ordin-ary, in-ter-esting*).
- Remember that there is a small group of two-syllabled nouns ending in *ce* which end in *se* when they become a verb (e.g. *practice/se; licence/se*).
- Learn rules of thumb:
  – *i* before *e* except after *c*, when the sound is *ee* (the only common exception is *seize*; words like *neighbour, weigh* and *weird* do not have a long *ee* sound)
  – double consonant, short vowel; single consonant, long vowel (e.g. ho*pp*ing and ho*p*ing)
  – adverbs end in *-ly* unless the adjective already ends in *-l*, then it's *-lly* (e.g. safely and successfu*lly*).

11 Read the newspaper articles below about teenagers' use of language.

Text A

A generation of teenagers risk making themselves unemployable because they are using a vocabulary of only 800 words a day. This is according to the UK government's first children's communication czar.

Furthermore, they are avoiding varied and complex words in favour of the abbreviated 'teenspeak' of text messsages, social networking sites and internet chat rooms. Jean Gross, the government's new adviser on childhood language development, is planning a national campaign to stop children failing in the classroom (and later in the workplace) because of their inability to express themselves.

She said, 'Teenagers are spending more time communicating through electronic media. We need to help today's teenagers understand the difference between their textspeak and the formal language they need to succeed in life – 800 words will not get you a job.'

By the age of 16 the majority of teenagers have developed a broad vocabulary of 40,000 words. Linguists have found, however, that many choose to limit themselves to a much smaller range of words in regular conversation. Their instinct is to simplify.

Ten million words of transcribed speech and 100,000 words gathered from teenagers' blogs have been analysed. The top 20 words used by teenagers – including 'yeah', 'no' and 'but' – account for about a third of all words used. A range of 1000 words is regarded as the minimum for foreigners to understand basic English.

Gross's campaign is set to target primary and secondary schools. She wants parents to limit children under the age of two to half an hour of television a day, because she says that it crowds out conversation, which is how vocabularies expand.

Adapted from an article by Sian Griffiths and Chris Gourlay, *The Sunday Times* 10th January 2010.

Text B

Predictive text messaging, a feature of mobile phones, changes the way children's brains develop and makes them more prone to make mistakes in their writing, according to a recent study. Children between the ages of 11 and 14 send an average of 20 text messages per week.

For a start, the results of using this function are often more a matter of miscommunication than communication, as the guesses made are often wrong. Although the user can scroll through a list of alternatives if the phone predicts the wrong word, they rarely do, and in fact 'book' has become an alternative slang term for 'cool'. The user may be able to type faster, but the result is less accurate. Previous research has shown that predictive texting makes people sloppy when it comes to vocabulary choice or spelling; commonly texted and commonly misspelt words are 'questionnaire', 'accommodate' and 'definitely'. Some scientists believe that predictive texting, which speeds up communication but makes it less reliable, leads to more impulsive and erroneous behaviour in life in general, and that as a result there could be repercussions for a whole generation.

Adapted from an article by Caroline Grant, *Mail Online*, 11th August 2009.

12 Look at these examples of paired punctuation marks used in Text A. Discuss with your partner what you think the difference is between the three types: commas, dashes and brackets. Tell your teacher what you have concluded.

  a *Jean Gross, the government's new adviser on childhood language development, is planning a national campaign*

  b *a national campaign to stop children failing in the classroom (and later in the workplace) because of their inability to express themselves.*

  c *The top 20 words used by teenagers – including 'yeah', 'no' and 'but' – account for about a third of all words used.*

> **TASK TIP**
>
> There are three ways in writing to create a **parenthesis** (a 'removable' phrase or clause which gives additional information without affecting the grammar of the main clause).
>
> ■ a pair of commas, e.g. *The new species, which the experts have yet to classify, includes …*
>
> ■ a pair of dashes, e.g. *The new species – which the experts have yet to classify – includes …*
>
> ■ a pair of brackets, e.g. *The new species (which the experts have yet to classify) includes …*
>
> You should use all of these in your own writing to provide range and variety of punctuation, and to suggest how separate from the main idea you wish the additional material to seem. Brackets are the strongest separation, and most rarely used; dashes are considered less formal than the other two methods and are less likely to be found in older writing.

113

13 a Reduce both texts in Activity **11** to a list of argument bullet points.

  b Give each article a suitable title.

  c Summarise the two points of view in one sentence each.

  d Circle the ideas in your Text A and Text B list that you disagree with.

  e Write next to the ideas you have circled how you would refute them.

14 a Write a plan for an article in response to the texts in Activity **11**, called *In defence of teenspeak*. You need at least **five** separate ideas and ways of developing and supporting them. Put them in the best order.

  b List possible first sentences for your piece.

  c Ask your partner to choose the best opening, justifying their choice.

KEY POINT

Some coursework assignments are based on a text containing facts, opinions and arguments. It should be a text containing several main ideas which are provocative and elicit a strong response from the reader. You are required to respond to the text by selecting, analysing and evaluating points from the material. You can also examine, where relevant, how language has been used to convey the ideas in a forceful or biased way.

TASK TIP

The first sentence of any writing or speaking, but especially an argument, is very important for engaging the reader/audience. An obvious or dull statement will not arouse interest in the topic or convey the passion needed to inspire confidence in your opinions. An effective opening could be:

■ an unexpected claim *(Technology is making humans more primitive.)*
■ a provocative statement *(We all lose control sometimes.)*
■ a succinct summary of a situation *(Global warming is responsible for most of the Earth's environmental problems.)*
■ a famous quotation *(All power corrupts, and absolute power corrupts absolutely.)*
■ a direct question *(How do you feel about the world your children will inherit?)*

Which type of opening is used in the texts in Activity **11**?

15 Discuss with your partner the weaknesses of the following openings for the argument titles given in brackets.

   a Water has many uses. (*Water is life*)

   b As with most questions, there are two sides to be considered. (*Capital punishment*)

   c Nobody who has a television could have not been horrified by the recent events. (*What are your views on the invention of television?*)

   d Many factors affect how we live today. (*Does life get better or worse?*)

   e I feel very very strongly about this topic. (*Is there such a thing as justice?*)

16 Using the suggestions for openings in the Task tip, think of more effective ways to start the compositions in Activity **15**. Share your ideas with the rest of the class.

17 The **discourse markers** *Furthermore* and *For a start* are used in the texts in Activity **11**.

What other words/phrases can be used to link paragraphs in argument writing? With your partner, make a list of:

   a those which continue the argument in the same direction

   b those which indicate a change to the other viewpoint.

KEY POINT

Structure is essential in argumentative writing as a device for convincing the audience; there should be a sense of logical development in the order of your points, and a connection between paragraphs. Common linking words/ phrases are *therefore, furthermore, in addition, on the other hand, however, on the contrary, nevertheless, finally.* (Avoid using only a list of numbers: *first, second, third,* and so on.) The function of these linking phrases is to continue the line of argument or to change to the opposing view. It is better not to change direction more than once in an argument, or you may confuse the reader. It is effective to begin your argument by mentioning the opposite view from your own, so that you can then refute it to strengthen your own case, which is then developed in the rest of the response.

18 With a partner, put the planning notes below into the most logical and effective sequence for an argument composition entitled *Money is the root of all evil*. Choose your first and last points especially carefully.

- reason for wars
- responsible for greed and envy
- gives people false values
- not distributed fairly
- gambling an addiction
- connected to politics – causes corruption
- rich people often unhappy
- cause of most crimes – drugs trade
- can destroy relationships.

TASK TIP

In a piece of argumentative writing the last point is the most important and should be the strongest part. (Think of lawyers summing up in court.) It needs to clinch the argument and leave the reader convinced – and the examiner impressed by the structure. Don't end randomly, fade away or weaken your argument by repetition. To conclude effectively, you might:

- refer back to an opening statement
- look into the future
- suggest a new angle
- make an original observation
- make a short definitive statement
- quote a famous saying
- make a humorous comment (if appropriate to the topic).

19 With a partner, expand the planning notes in Activity **18** by adding details for each one, including examples, references to people or events, statistics or well-known sayings.

KEY POINT

Any argument title can be argued from either viewpoint, so if you find you cannot get enough points for the side you first try to plan, consider switching to the alternative view. Remember it is not your knowledge or opinions which are being judged, but your ability to construct a relevant, focused, varied, supported, linked piece of continuous writing, in an appropriate style and with an effective sequence, for the title and type of writing you have chosen or been asked to do.

20 Your plan supports the argument that money has a harmful influence in the world, but it would be equally possible to present a case for its benefits.

As a class, **brainstorm** on the board the opposite point of view, for a debate speech entitled *Money makes the world go round*. Agree on a sequence for the points and add the linking words/phrases you would use at the beginning of each paragraph.

21 Read the passage below, which is an editorial from a national daily newspaper.

22 Discuss as a class why newspapers have editorials. What sorts of issues do they comment on, and why?

TASK TIP

An editorial expresses and argues the viewpoint of the editor, and it represents the view of the newspaper owner and the opinions of the newspaper as a whole, which are determined by its political stance. It is a kind of speech and the same as a spoken argument in form, aim and use of rhetorical style and emotive language.

Safe landings
Nothing can replace old-fashioned pilot skills

Air travel has become, in the space of a few short years, a commodity which is within the reach of the vast majority of the population. And even as low-cost airlines have relentlessly driven down costs, so technological improvements have improved safety so far that, in Europe and North America at least, accidents have become extremely rare. But as aircraft systems have increased in sophistication, unwise observers have questioned whether there is really a need for two highly (and expensively) trained pilots in the cockpit at all.

Two examples of outstanding airmanship have, however, given dramatic evidence that, in a rare and extreme emergency, it is the ice-cool reflexes and professional skill of the pilots which have meant the difference between life and horrific death for many hundreds of people. When a flock of Canada geese destroyed both engines of US Airways flight 1549, less than three minutes into a flight from New York's La Guardia airport, the aircraft was still so low that no airfield was within range. With no power and no altitude for manoeuvre, Captain Chesley

Sullenberger calmly ditched the aircraft in the River Hudson, making the most perfect on-water landing ever achieved by a jet airliner. All 155 on board were safely rescued: Captain Sullenberger was the last to leave, having twice walked the length of the cabin to ensure that no passenger remained on board the sinking aircraft. Not for nothing was he rapidly dubbed the hero of the 'Miracle on the Hudson'.

Bird strikes are the most common cause of in-flight incident, and it was a flock of starlings which nearly brought disaster to Ryanair flight 4102 when it was seconds away from landing at Rome's Ciampino airport. More than 90 individual birds impacted the aircraft, destroying the port engine and landing gear and seriously damaging the other – at an altitude of 50 feet. With only seconds in which to react, the pilots decided not to attempt to go around and assess the damage – the normal procedure, but which would have led to certain catastrophe. Instead, with effectively no power and damaged undercarriage, the captain slammed the aircraft onto the ground, and then wrestled it back onto the runway after

Captain Sullenberger

the damaged landing gear made it slew to the left. Again, every occupant walked away.

In each of these instances, and countless others, it was human judgement which saved the plane and its occupants, and no amount of fancy electronics will ever replace the split-second reactions and advanced skills of an experienced pilot.

23 With your partner, find rhetorical devices (expressions used to influence the reader) in the text in Activity **21**. Find examples of the following:

   a   words that evoke strong emotion

   b   words that have dramatic effect

   c   unusual word order for emphasis

   d   alliteration for impact

   e   extremes, absolutes and negatives for tension

   f   words that steer the reader's response.

> **TASK TIP**
>
> To argue effectively you must be familiar with the typical features of **rhetoric**. In addition to the devices mentioned in Activity **23**, these include:
>
> - triple structures – to emphasise scope or variety (e.g. *Before, during, after the event*)
> - questions – to engage the reader (*Do we really believe that …?*)
> - exclamations – to suggest strong feeling (*Heaven forbid!*)
> - repetition – to emphasise key idea (*All that matters is education, education, education*)
> - hypotheticals – to make the strongest possible case by discussing the best- or worst-case scenario (*If this were to happen* or *Unless we do something*)
> - negatives – to stress difficulty and danger (*no easy task* or *not one person*)
> - intensifiers – for emphasis (*only, extremely, absolutely*)
> - lists – to impress with number (*men, women, children, babies*)
> - elevated diction – to make speaker seem educated (*eradicate* instead of *get rid of*)
> - **antithesis** – for ironic or dramatic contrast (*'One small step for man, one giant leap for mankind'*).
>
> You should not use excessively emotive language, however, as this can make your case sound more like biased propaganda than a considered and reasoned opinion based on evidence.

24 Plan a response to oppose that expressed by the editorial in Activity **21**, in which you argue that human beings are and always have been the main cause of accidents and disasters, and that machines are generally more reliable. The title is *To err is human*. Decide on your examples and evidence, and the order of your points. Write your first and final sentences, then read them to the class to judge their effectiveness.

 Further practice

   a   Write your argumentative article *To err is human*, planned in Activity **24**.

   b   Imagine you are the editor of the weekly newspaper in which Activity **2** Text C was published. Write an editorial in which you tell your readers how they should react to the news report.

   c   Find a report of an event or comments published in a newspaper or magazine on a topic about which you have a strong view. Write to the letters page of the publication to present your argument. Remember to use evidence to support your case and to refer to the original report or article. Write about 300 words. Begin *Dear Editor…*

Unit 12: Continuous Writing

This unit looks at creating character and empathy through the use of voice, viewpoint and dialogue in narrative, for an exam composition or coursework assignment.

KEY POINT

Dialogue can be used effectively at the beginning or end of a narrative, to engage interest or to provide an ironic twist. It is also a way of providing drama, tension and climax within a narrative.

It is pointless, however, for everyday comments to be given as dialogue, as this would simply hold up the story without contributing anything to it. Dialogue also becomes ineffective if used so much that your writing becomes a playscript, with no intervening narrative.

If used appropriately and sparingly, however, speech can help to convey characters' personalities and relationships, especially if the characters speak in a different style from one another.

In the story in Activity **1** the characters speak in the same style but their opinions, as expressed through dialogue, are what differentiate them.

1 Read this extract from the end of a short story about an old man and a young woman playing a game called 'Go'.

2 Contribute to a class discussion about these questions.

   a The story could be described as allegorical. What features fit this definition?

   b What physical description would you use to create realistic characters?

   c What can we infer about the characters' views on life from the way they speak?

   d What does the use of dialogue contribute to the passage?

   e At what points in a narrative is dialogue likely to be effective?

3 With a partner, remind yourselves of the rules of setting out dialogue by looking at the text in Activity **1**. Your teacher will write them on the board using contributions from the class.

The two players place their stones on the board using only their fingers, not their thumbs. It is necessary to think very carefully about where to put the stones, and to hold them properly. A long time passes between each move. They do not place the stones in the squares; this is not a game like chess or draughts, but on the corners where the lines meet.

The old man worries about the way the young woman is playing the game. He does not recognise her style, her strategy. He can't read her face; he does not understand her. Sometimes, he thinks that he does not understand the world around him any longer.

'The way I think about the game,' says the woman, 'is that it is a series of steps for getting what I want.' Again, the old man is surprised. For him, the game is a way of life, life itself, and not a model of life. He worries about the dignity of the game, the elegance of the board. She worries about getting points.

'There is no more beauty any longer. Everything is science and rules. Everything is about winning. Nothing is about playing,' he says.

'What sense does a game have if you don't win?'

'The playing is the sense,' replies the man.

People have been playing this game for 3000 years. Sometimes, the two players think, this game will last 3000 years. The man feels like he has been playing Go for 3000 years.

'This game was invented by generals. They used it to work out strategies for war. They used the stones to map out positions,' he tells her. 'And then they decided that it was better to have a game than have a war.'

'Are we at war now?' she asks. He wants to say no, but does not know how to reply.

TASK TIP

Setting out dialogue in a narrative:

- Start a new line or paragraph for a change of speaker.
- Use double inverted commas at the beginning and end of the speech (in handwritten work; single inverted commas in typed work).
- Use a full stop, comma, question mark or exclamation mark at the end of every speech (and inside the final inverted commas).
- Use a capital letter to begin a speech, even in the middle of a sentence.
- Use the same punctuation within a speech as you would for ordinary sentences.

Characters in dialogue speak alternately. A new line signifies a change of speaker, so it is not necessary to keep writing a speech verb and the name or pronoun of the character for every speech, as is shown in the passage in Activity **1**. This speeds up the pace and makes the dialogue sound more dramatic and spontaneous. Note that thoughts are represented within speech marks as if they were utterances.

4   Think of an incident which could be expressed as dialogue in a science-fiction narrative. Write the dialogue and read it to the class.

5   Did you use the verb *said* in the last activity? With your partner, list all the more precise and interesting verbs (e.g. *shouted* or *muttered*) you can think of for reporting speech. These also help to convey character.

'There is another story,' says the young woman. 'Go began when people threw stones to tell fortunes.'

'Will this game tell our fortune?'

'It is better to play a game than try to tell the future,' she says, and he is surprised again. This time he is surprised by how wise her words are.

'The future is a game that has already started. The future is waiting to see who the winner is,' he says. 'Every move you make determines what will happen in the future.' They play Go for six months. At the end of six months, they know that their final game is close. The final game will decide who is the winner, and who the loser.

'A game is a metaphor for life.'

'No, life is a metaphor for a game.'

They cannot agree; but it is not necessary. They both look at the Go board in silence. It looks like a work of art, and also a scientific document. It is a map, a map of the game they played, and a map of their thoughts.

'Change is a necessary part of life,' thinks the man.

'Playing is as important as winning,' thinks the woman.

They start to play their final game.

From *A Game of Go*, by Chris Rose, British Council's *Learn English*

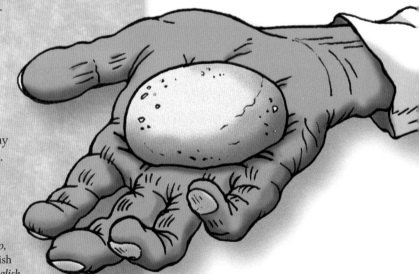

6 With a partner, make up convincing spoken dialogue for each of the situations below. Try to make the two characters talk in different ways to differentiate their personalities and feelings. Give them three short speeches each. Read your dialogue in role to the class for them to guess which picture it relates to.

TASK TIP

It is difficult to make dialogue sound realistic: on the one hand it needs to convey information necessary for the plot and to reveal character, but on the other it needs to sound like natural speech. It sounds artificial if the name of the interlocutor (person having a conversation) is frequently used, as in real life people rarely use the name of the person they are speaking to (unless they are telling them off!)

Colloquial language and abbreviations can be used in dialogue, and you may wish to give a character an accent or dialect, as dialogue is meant to reflect spoken not written language. It is not a good idea, however, to use swear words or incomprehensible jargon in compositions written for assessment purposes, even for the purpose of conveying character.

7 Read the text below, which is in reported speech.

> Diwan thought that it was a bad idea to steal the chemicals from the school science laboratory and he said so to his friend Sanjeet, who was busy hiding packets of them in his school bag. Sanjeet's expressed view was that no one would notice they were missing and they could have some fun with them after school. When asked what they were for, he said that he planned to mix them together and set fire to them to make some spectacular smells, colours and noises. Diwan warned him that if he didn't know what he was doing chemicals could be very dangerous, especially when mixed together, and that it wasn't worth the risk of injury or of being caught for stealing. The aggressive response he got was that he was no fun, and much too timid and boring, and that if he wasn't going to join in then Sanjeet would find someone else to hang out with, that day and for ever.

8 Turn the passage above into direct speech. Set out the dialogue correctly and choose speech verbs carefully to convey character, avoiding the use of *said*. Swap your work with a partner to correct and give a mark out of 10 for accurate punctuation.

9 Read the two paragraphs below, which give two different third-person viewpoints in the retelling of a familiar fairy tale.

Text A

One day a girl is asked by her mother to take some food to her sick grandmother who lives in a cottage in the woods. She is forbidden to speak to anyone on the way or leave the path, but she disobeys and tells a wolf where she is going, and then wastes time wandering about picking flowers. When she gets to her grandmother's house she doesn't notice that her grandmother is being impersonated by the wolf, even though she talks to it. The wolf has eaten her grandmother and is about to eat the girl, and she is only saved by the intervention of a woodcutter who happens to be passing. He cuts open the wolf and frees the old woman.

Text B

One day a mother orders her young daughter to take a food basket to her sick grandmother, who lives far away in the middle of a dangerous forest. She doesn't want to go and is frightened by the idea of making such a journey on her own. While walking, she is approached by an large and evil wolf, who tricks her into telling him where she is going and why. By the time the unsuspecting girl arrives at her grandmother's house, the wolf has killed the poor old woman, put on her clothes, and is sitting in her bed. The girl feels something is wrong and asks her 'grandmother' questions about her strange appearance. Suddenly the wolf leaps out to attack the terrified girl. Her screams bring the help of a nearby woodcutter and both she and her grandmother are saved.

10 a Which fairy tale is being written about in Texts A and B, and what is the moral of the tale?

  b Which of the two texts is more sympathetic to the main character?

  c How has the reader been made to feel sympathy in this text?

11 Choose another well-known fairy or folk tale and write a paragraph plot **synopsis** as the first-person viewpoint of someone other than the main character (e.g. an ugly sister in *Cinderella*). Read it to the class and ask them to guess the story and the character.

12 Read the synopsis of a short story set in Columbia.

Aurelio Escovar is told by his son that the mayor has arrived, demanding to have a tooth taken out that has been causing him pain for several days and nights. At first the dentist doesn't want to help the mayor because he blames him for the death of 20 local men, but then he realises that this gives him the power and opportunity to punish the mayor. He extracts the infected tooth brutally, without giving him any anaesthetic, making the mayor suffer and cry. When the mayor leaves he is rude to the dentist to show that he is back to his normal bullying self and not at all grateful. The dentist has achieved nothing except to make an even greater enemy of the mayor.

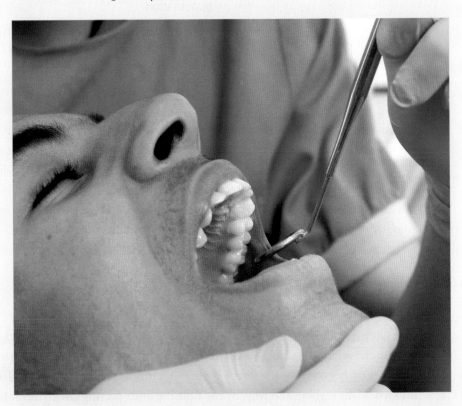

13 a Discuss in class which character you feel empathy for and why.

  b Rewrite the plot summary in a way that changes the viewpoint and positions the reader to feel sympathy for the other character.

14 Listen to the dialogue, an extract from a short story, read aloud (by classmates or your teacher), with different voices for the two speakers.

123

'You write books?' he asked.

'Yes.'

'Writin' books is OK,' he said. 'It's what I call a skilled trade. I'm in a skilled trade too. The folks I despise is them that spend all their lives doin' crummy old routine job with no skill in 'em at all. You see what I mean?'

'Yes.'

'The secret of life,' he said, 'is to become very very good at somethin' that's very very 'ard to do.'

'Like you,' I said.

'Exactly. You and me both.'

'What makes you think that I'm any good at my job?' I asked. 'There's an awful lot of bad writers around.'

'You wouldn't be drivin' about in a car like this if you weren't no good at it,' he answered. 'It must've cost a tidy packet, this little job.'

'It wasn't cheap.'

'What can she do flat out?' he asked.

'Two hundred kilometres an hour,' I told him.

'I'll bet she won't do it.'

'I'll bet she will'.

'All car makers are liars,' he said. 'You can buy any car you like and it'll never do what the makers say it will in the ads.'

'This one will.'

'Open 'er up then and prove it,' he said. 'Go on, guv'nor, open 'er right up and let's see what she'll do.'

From 'The Hitch-Hiker', in *Into the Wind*, by Roald Dahl.

15 Discuss in class how the voices and speeches differ, and what their way of speaking conveys about the two characters.

TASK TIP

Sometimes words used in direct speech need to be stressed to clarify tone and meaning. In type or print this is shown by putting the word or syllable in italics. As this device cannot be used in handwritten work, you can underline the stressed parts instead. The convention for showing that a character is shouting is to put their speech in capital letters. Note that question marks and exclamation marks are used singly, one per utterance, and not both together (except in comic books).

16 Change each use of a speech verb (*asked*, *said*, *told*, *answered*) to a different verb, and one which conveys an appropriate tone of voice and sense of character.

17 Imagine what each of the following types of character might say on receiving a gift of the latest version of a smartphone. Create a different voice for each.

  a   a middle-aged secretary

  b   an IT geek

  c   an elderly technophobe

  d   a teenager

18 Read the opening of a well-known gothic short story, below.

19 Work in small groups on the passage and present your feedback to the class for the following questions and tasks.

  a   What is the effect of the four short speeches by the narrator?

  b   What is the effect of the lack of response by the other character, the signalman?

'Halloa! Below there!'

When he heard a voice thus calling to him, he was standing at the door of his box, with a flag in his hand, furled round its short pole. One would have thought, considering the nature of the ground, that he could not have doubted from what quarter the voice came; but, instead of looking up to where I stood on the top of the steep cutting nearly over his head, he turned himself about and looked down the Line. There was something remarkable in his manner of doing so, though I could not have said, for my life, what. But, I know it was remarkable enough to attract my notice, even though his figure was foreshortened and shadowed, down in the deep trench, and mine was high above him, so steeped in the glow of an angry sunset that I had shaded my eyes with my hand before I saw him at all.

'Halloa! Below!'

From looking down the Line, he turned himself about again, and, raising his eyes, saw my figure high above him.

'Is there any path by which I can come down and speak to you?'

He looked up at me without replying, and I looked down at him without pressing him too soon with a repetition of my idle question. Just then, there came a vague vibration in the earth and air, quickly changing into a violent pulsation, and an oncoming rush that caused me to start back, as though it had force to draw me down. When such vapour as rose to my height from this rapid train, had passed me and was skimming away over the landscape, I looked down again, and saw him re-furling the flag he had shown while the train went by.

I repeated my inquiry. After a pause, during which he seemed to regard me with fixed attention, he motioned with his rolled-up flag towards a point on my level, some two or three hundred yards distant. I called down to him, 'All right!' and made for that point. There, by dint of looking closely about me, I found a rough zig-zag descending path notched out: which I followed.

The cutting was extremely deep, and unusually precipitate. It was made through a clammy stone that became oozier and wetter as I went down. For these reasons, I found the way long enough to give me time to recall a singular air of reluctance or compulsion with which he had pointed out the path.

When I came down low enough upon the zig-zag descent, to see him again, I saw that he was standing between the rails on the way by which the train had lately passed, in an attitude as if he were waiting for me to appear. He had his left hand at his chin, and that left elbow rested on his right hand crossed over his breast. His attitude was one of such expectation and watchfulness, that I stopped a moment, wondering at it.

c   Summarise the setting, including time and weather, and comment on its
     effect.

d   What can be inferred about the character of the narrator?

e   Study the description of the signalman. Describe the character it conveys,
     giving quotations in support, and comment on what the reader expects of
     such a character.

f   How would you describe the atmosphere? List the words which have
     contributed to the atmosphere.

g   List the ways, with examples, in which a feeling of tension has been created.

h   What role is played by the passing train?

i   The opening foreshadows how the story will develop. What do you predict
     will happen? Give evidence for your predictions.

j   Try to explain how the story would be different so far if narrated in the
     third person.

I resumed my downward way, and, stepping out upon the level of the railroad and drawing nearer to him, saw
that he was a dark sallow man, with a dark beard and rather heavy eyebrows. His post was in as solitary and
dismal a place as ever I saw. On either side, a dripping-wet wall of jagged stone, excluding all view but a strip
of sky; the perspective one way, only a crooked prolongation of this great dungeon; the shorter perspective in
the other direction, terminating in a gloomy red light, and the gloomier entrance to a black tunnel, in whose
massive architecture there was a barbarous, depressing, and forbidding air. So little sunlight ever found its
way to this spot, that it had an earthy deadly smell; and so much cold wind rushed through it, that it struck
chill to me, as if I had left the natural world.

Before he stirred, I was near enough to him to have touched him. Not even then removing his eyes from mine,
he stepped back one step, and lifted his hand.

This was a lonesome post to occupy (I said), and it had riveted my attention when I looked down from up
yonder. A visitor was a rarity, I should suppose; not an unwelcome rarity, I hoped? In me, he merely saw a man
who had been shut up
within narrow limits all
his life, and who, being
at last set free, had a
newly-awakened interest
in these great works. To
such purpose I spoke to
him; but I am far from
sure of the terms I used,
for, besides that I am not
happy in opening any
conversation, there was
something in the man
that daunted me.

From 'The Signalman', in *Stories
of Ourselves*, by Charles Dickens.

20 Write your own opening to a first-person horror short story, using the idea of two characters meeting for the first time in a strange place. Use some dialogue, and some of the techniques and ideas from the passage in Activity **18**, to convey character, voice and viewpoint. Write about 300 words.

➕ Further practice

a Complete the short story you began in Activity **20**, for exam practice or as a first draft for a coursework assignment.

b Write a modern version of a well-known fairy tale, containing dialogue. Think about character stereotypes, and clichéd situations and language, and try to subvert them and work against reader expectations to create humour (e.g. a modern version of *Cinderella* could feature a help-line and a rock star instead of a fairy godmother and a prince, or end with the twist that one of the ugly sisters is chosen rather than Cinderella).

c A person suffering from amnesia (memory loss) has been found wandering in the centre of a major city. The only clues to identity are the items below:

- local restaurant receip
- photo of two teenagers
- medication for allergies
- car keys
- theatre programme
- packet of chewing gum

- handkerchief with initial *M*
- wedding ring
- street map of the city
- large sum in cash
- gold watch
- sunglasses.

You are the detective asked to put together a profile of the person and their recent movements, in the hope that a relative will come forward to identify them after a description is issued. You may make inferences from and add details to the objects listed. You can also add a description of what the person was wearing.

Part 5:
Speaking and Listening

Unit 13: Giving a talk and conducting a dialogue

This unit helps you to deliver a prepared individual talk and to engage in dialogue for different purposes, including roleplays or interviews.

1   Choose a sport or game that you know something about and prepare to answer the following questions orally. Work with your partner to ask each other these questions after you have thought about your answers.

   a   Which activity have you chosen, and why?

   b   What are the aims of the activity?

   c   What environment, equipment, clothing and facilities are needed to take part in this activity?

   d   What is the attraction of the activity?

   e   What do you know about the background/history of the activity? For example, when did it start? Which countries is it mainly associated with?

2   With a partner, turn the set of rules below into a clear explanation of how the game of cricket is played.

The 'rules' of cricket

* You have two sides: one out in the field and one in.

* Each player that's in the side that's in goes out and when he's out he comes in and the next player goes in until he's out.

* When they are all out, the side that's out comes in and the side that's been in goes out and tries to get those coming in out.

* Sometimes you get players still in and not out.

* When both sides have been in and out, including the not outs, that's the end of the match.

3   Rehearse silently an explanation of how to perform the activity you chose in Activity **1**. Use language that is precise and concise, but not too technical. Avoid sentences that are too long or complicated. Be prepared to answer questions about the rules of the game.

After you have had five minutes to prepare, your teacher will pick students to talk to the rest of the class, and the class will ask questions.

4   Read or listen to someone reading the website article about computer games.

Games Children Play

| Games Home | New Games | **Games Life** | Help | Log in | Sign up |

Once upon a time, if you said that kids were playing games, it probably meant some make-believe with guns or dolls, or maybe they were playing a board-game like Monopoly, or backgammon, or for the hyper-intelligent, chess.

That all changed with the invention of the computer – or rather, not the invention, which was way back in the Second World War, but the creation of small, cheap computers. From then on, and for all of my lifetime, playing games has meant playing 'computer games'. I hope you can hear my inverted commas, because most of them are actually played on consoles, or tablets, or smartphones, but they are all based on 'computer' technology.

Some people – mostly older people – think that computer games are always violent and destructive. I guess they may have seen that old favourite, Space Invaders, where brave kids protect their helpless parents from destruction at the hands of endless legions of little square aliens. Others a bit more tech-savvy are probably thinking of Grand Theft Auto, having looked over their son's shoulder and seen him systematically slaughtering innocent people and getting bonus points for the degree of violence employed. At least, that's how parents interpret it.

What they don't get is that almost computer games are fundamentally harmless and actually educational. They are generations more advanced than clunky old Space Invaders. They encourage rapid thinking, dexterity, hand-eye co-ordination, problem-solving, tactical decision-taking – and, increasingly, they require highly-developed social skills, such as diplomacy and negotiation.

What parents can't see and don't know (because they don't ask) is that many – most – of the games that kids play now are not stand-alone 'First Person Shooters' (as the geeks technically call them), but a whole new phenomenon – real-time, online worlds in which millions of real human players interact with one another in dozens of different ways.

Officially called 'MMO' games – for Massively Multiplayer Online – they bring a whole new dimension to gaming. They can be of any kind – medieval, modern, science fiction – in any world you can imagine. They can be about making cities or making war, solving mysteries or creating them. But the key point is that you are playing with real people – from all over the world, people you could never meet in real life – and because of that, the game is different every time. It is truly creative, in that together you make everything happen. You use your social skills to build teams and achieve your goals together, whatever they are.

Furthermore, it is no longer true that only boys play computer games (if it ever was!). Multi-player games especially appeal to girls because of the social aspect, and because there are so many which are about building communities – think of the Sims – or about building families and educating them. Actually, you also find many girls in medieval fantasy worlds as well, adventuring, discovering, taking on challenges. Gender roles are becoming less stereotyped all the time.

So that's what playing games means to most kids today. Tomorrow, who knows?

5 With your partner, find evidence that this passage is in the style of colloquial spoken rather than formal written English.

> **KEY POINT**
>
> Spoken English in an informal register is likely to contain the following:
>
> - idioms and colloquialisms
> - fashionable expressions
> - contractions
> - use of *You* and *I*
> - short sentences
> - monosyllabic vocabulary
> - *And*, *But* and *Or* to start sentences
> - acronyms
> - afterthoughts signified by dashes
> - asides
> - exclamations
> - non-sentences
> - simple grammatical structures
> - active rather than passive verbs.

6 What questions would you want to ask the writer of the article about computer games after listening to the talk? Write a list of questions. Compare it with your partner's.

7 Comment on the effect on the listener of someone starting a talk in each of the ways listed below.

   a *Erm … I'm not really sure what I'm going to talk about, but my favourite pastime is probably fishing … I think.*

   b *I am a leading expert in computer graphics, so listen and I'll tell you all about the subject, at length and in great detail.*

   c *Sub-atomic particles can be subsumed into hadrons and leptons, but spin and sense are fundamental criteria for any hierarchical categorisation matrix construct.*

   d *Before I start, I need to explain my life history and how I came to be involved in recycling.*

   e *I'm sure you feel the same way as I do about spiders. I mean, they're just really spooky, right?*

8 With a partner, write in two columns a *Do* and *Don't* list for how to deliver a talk. Share it with the class and form a combined list for the classroom wall.

KEY POINT

You need to be clear and concise in your talk, and a balance needs to be kept:

- Sound enthusiastic but not obsessive.
- Be knowledgeable but not tedious.
- Use precise vocabulary but not jargon.
- Use interesting vocabulary but not words you don't know the meaning of.
- Use varied but not over-complex grammar.
- Be engaging but not too casual.
- Talk neither too fast nor too slowly.
- Talk enough but not too much.
- Provide an introduction, but only a very brief one.
- Make it clear when you've finished, but not by repeating anything you've already said.

Speaking and listening skills include actions as well as words; body language shows attitude and confidence level, and sends either positive or negative messages to the audience. For example folding your arms may make you seem defensive, and fiddling with something or waving your arms can be distracting.

9   You are going to prepare a talk on a leisure pastime or interest. With a partner, agree on the logical order in which to answer the following questions, and number them to provide a structure for your talk.

- How long have I had this hobby?
- What is its exact definition?
- What equipment/environment is necessary?
- What memorable/successful/disastrous moments have occurred?
- What kind of people share my hobby / how common is it?
- How do I see my future with regard to this hobby?
- What caused me to take up this hobby?
- What is its physical/emotional appeal?
- What are its difficulties and drawbacks?
- How do my family/friends regard my hobby?

131

KEY POINT

Your audience should be gripped from the start. Be personal and passionate about your topic, as well as informative. Although you need to give accurate facts, your talk must sound genuinely personal and not just something you have researched.

Remember that listeners may know nothing about the subject, so don't assume too much or use too many technical words. Your aim is to be interesting, varied, informative, memorable and original. Humour, sparingly and appropriately used, can contribute to an enjoyable and successful presentation.

TASK TIP

Do you have a speech habit that you aren't aware of? Do you clear your throat often, rely on using fillers (e.g. *er*, *um* or *like*), use certain words or phrases repeatedly (e.g. *you know* or *OK*) or overuse a particular adjective (e.g. *amazing*)?

Ask your partner to point out any unconscious and irritating habits so that you can work on eliminating them from your speech.

10 Now that you have a structure, choose the topic for your talk.

   a List the points you need to research.

   b Indicate where you think you can find the information.

   c Prepare your opening statement on the topic. It should be one medium-length paragraph (about 70 words) which immediately engages the listener.

11 With your partner, take turns to deliver your opening statements on your chosen topics. Afterwards, help each other to improve delivery and raise the level of audience interest.

12 With your partner, try to predict the questions the examiner might ask after your talk, and think about appropriate responses. This preparation will make it less likely that you will be caught out by an unexpected question.

13 Listen to a recording of a talk and the following discussion. Give it a mark and a supporting comment from the band descriptors in the mark scheme for your exam syllabus.

14 Giving your talk.

   a Research the topic that you chose in Activity 9, using your list from Activity 10a and your introduction from Activity 11.

   b Prepare your cue cards.

   c With your partner, practise your talks and play the role of examiner in the subsequent discussion. Check that the talk is the right length (three to four minutes long), and adjust if necessary.

   d You are now ready to be recorded performing your talk to the class or for your teacher.

KEY POINT

You must not follow a script or try to recite from memory. You will feel more confident if you prepare a list of headings on a cue card, relating to the different aspects of the topic, which you can refer to discreetly. This will enable you to show that you can present facts, ideas and opinions in a sustained, cohesive order, but at the same time appear to be talking naturally.

A limited quantity of illustrative material is allowed, so you could use realia as visual aids, or project slides, but these should be aids for your audience rather than text to be read by you. You should make eye contact with your audience as often as possible, and not pace up and down or look above their heads.

15 With your partner, discuss the four cartoons below, then answer the following questions for each picture.

    a   What is the location?

    b   Who is in the picture and what can we guess about them?

    c   What is the situation; what has just happened?

    d   What is likely to happen next?

    e   What do you think the characters are thinking/feeling?

KEY POINT

Dialogue is the most common form of spoken communication, and you can demonstrate this skill in your own person or as a roleplay. Typical dialogues have the following purposes:

- discussing
- complaining
- advising
- persuading
- questioning/answering
- explaining
- requesting
- apologising.

16 With your partner, discuss what the two characters in each picture could be saying to each other. Allocate and practise speaking the parts of the characters. Choose your best dialogue to perform to the rest of the class.

17 In Activity **16** the dialogues are between strangers. Choose one of the following situations and, with your partner, conduct an imaginary phone conversation between friends. You should each speak **five** times, so first agree who will start, how the dialogue will develop and how it will conclude.

- Your friend has phoned you because he or she has lost the instructions for your English homework. Explain what was set and give advice on how to approach it.

- You think your friend is spending too much time studying and needs a break. Persuade your friend to join you and some other friends for an evening out.

- You have received a fine for a library book which you borrowed but then lent to a friend. Phone the friend to ask what has happened to the book, complain that it was not returned on time and ask them to remedy the situation.

KEY POINT

In a role-play situation you need to show that you can converse confidently and naturally, using a range of appropriate vocabulary and grammatical structures. You need to demonstrate that you can listen to and respond appropriately to the contributions of others in a range of situations. You should take into account the relationship between the speakers in terms of relative ages, official positions and whether you have met before. Generally, you will use longer words and sentences for more formal situations.

18 Did you express yourself differently in Activities **16** and **17**? How does talking to a friend differ from talking to a stranger?

With your partner, discuss the differences between formal and informal spoken English, then copy out and complete the grid started below.

Formal	Informal
precise vocabulary	*colloquial expressions*

19 With your partner, choose (or your teacher will allocate) one of the following situations for role play dialogues of about three minutes, to be practised and performed to the rest of the class.

a A colleague explains over the phone how to do something, and answers the queries about the process.

b A radio or television presenter interviews someone who has discovered or invented something, and asks what difference it will make.

c A prosecuting lawyer cross-examines a defendant in court.

d A newspaper reporter questions a victim of, or witness to, a serious crime.

e A headteacher asks a student why their academic performance has suddenly and drastically declined.

TASK TIP

In a pair-based activity of this sort, you should:

■ adopt and maintain an appropriate tone of voice

■ respond promptly to changes of direction in mood and subject matter

■ develop ideas, give opinions, defend points of view, initiate new material

■ use a range of language

■ communicate clearly, fluently and effectively.

You are also expected to use standard English, to contribute relevantly, and to respect the other's views by acknowledging their questions, suggestions and reservations. Your aim is to arrive at a satisfactory conclusion to the dialogue.

20 Work with a partner. A magazine has sent a reporter to interview a national or international celebrity who is visiting your home town. Choose anyone whom you know a little bit about, and decide which of you will play the celebrity and which the reporter. Plan and practise (but do *not* script) the interview in the form of a question-and-answer dialogue.

Make sure that the interviewee says more than the interviewer and gives fully developed responses to the questions. Record the interview, which can then be played to the rest of the class for comment and assessment.

21 In groups of four to six, you are going to prepare for job interview roleplays. Decide which two of you will be interviewers; the rest will be applicants for the jobs. Your teacher will give each group one of the job advertisements shown on page 136.

You will be assessed on your speaking and listening skills throughout the activity. Work through the following stages:

a   The interviewers consult with each other and draw up lists of qualifications and characteristics which the successful applicant for the job must have.

b   Simultaneously, the job applicants individually write application letters, using false names, to be given to the interviewers by the teacher. Applicants can make up qualifications and experience!

c   The interviewers decide on the questions to be asked at interview, who will ask which questions, and in which order.

d   At the same time, the applicants individually try to predict the questions they will be asked and prepare answers to them. They also plan questions they wish to ask the interviewers.

e   The interviewers rank the application letters (based on style and accuracy of English, and appropriateness and persuasiveness of content) and announce the order for the interviews.

f   The applicants take turns to be interviewed. The teacher and rest of the class observe and make evaluation notes.

g   The applicants reflect on the role play and individually write comments on how they think they performed personally, and on the performance of the interviewers (e.g. did the interviewers make them want the job, put them at ease, and ask relevant and acceptable questions?).

h   At the same time, the interviewers confer and decide who to offer the job to, and why, and prepare debriefing comments for all the applicants.

i   The applicants give their feedback comments in turn.

j   The interviewers announce their decision, giving their reasons and offering advice for the unsuccessful applicants.

k   The successful applicant says whether he or she accepts the job, giving reasons why or why not.

l   The class are invited to give their comments on the whole interview role play and to make constructive criticisms of the performances.

m   The teacher says whether he or she thinks the right outcome was achieved and comments on the speaking and listening performances of all those involved, referring to the exam marking criteria and grades.

DYNAMIC SALES EXECUTIVES

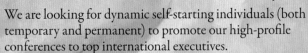

required for
International Conference Producers

We are looking for dynamic self-starting individuals (both temporary and permanent) to promote our high-profile conferences to top international executives.

Suitable candidates will need good communications skills, some knowledge of MS® Office and an excellent telephone manner.

An excellent remuneration package will be offered to the right candidate.

Please write in confidence to:

The Human Resources Manager
Global Conferences
10 Loveday Street, Johannesburg

Leading Travel Industry
Publication ...

invites applicants for the
following vacancy:

Junior Designer

Responsibilities include:

- assisting in the design and layout of monthly publications
- supporting design on other marketing projects
- liaising with printers

Requirements:

- ability to be creative and work independently
- ability to work to strict deadlines
- ability to work as part of a team

Please send your CV and a letter to:

Jorge Salas
Paseo Colon 220
Buenos Aires

Red Star Shipping Company Ltd

Receptionist / Booking Clerk

We have a vacancy for the above position to work in our prestigious offices in Singapore.

The candidate will speak and write both English and Chinese. His/her duties will be answering the telephone, taking messages, making reservations, dealing with clients both personally and by telephone, working in Microsoft® Word, Excel, etc., typing quotations and letters, filing, etc.

Please send your CV and a photo to:
Red Star Co Ltd

4545 Changi Boulevard, Singapore

ADMINISTRATIVE ASSISTANT

General office administration:

- Excellent computer skills, including word processing and spreadsheets
- Excellent written and spoken English
- Some experience with Internet programmes
- Mailshots to potential clients
- Database management
- Maintaining client relationships
- Some market research required
- Excellent telephone manner
- Enthusiastic, self-motivated, able to work independently

Please send CV with photo to:

Khalid Mahmud   Amibiostat AG
P.O. Box 1600   Abu Dhabi

➕ Further practice

a Write two versions of a short dialogue between a teacher and a former student who have met in the street of their home town a year after the student left school to go to university. Version A should be formal and Version B should be informal.

b Listen to an interview with a politician or spokesperson for an organisation, on radio or television. Evaluate the performance of both speakers by giving them a mark out of 10 for their speaking and listening skills. Is the interviewer trying to bully the interviewee? Does the interviewee actually answer the interviewer's questions? Who 'wins' the dialogue?

c Prepare speeches to fill the missing parts in the dialogue below between a hotel manager and a dissatisfied guest, to be performed in class with a partner reading the part of 'the manager'.

Manager	Good morning! How can I be of service?
Guest	…
Manager	I'm very sorry to hear that. What exactly is the problem?
Guest	…
Manager	No, I'm sure that can't be the case. I think you must have misunderstood.
Guest	…
Manager	Really? I find that very surprising, but I will look into it immediately.
Guest	…
Manager	Of course. I will let you know as soon as I have talked to the conference organiser.
Guest	…
Manager	I understand that you feel very strongly, but I hope that it won't come to that.
Guest	…
Manager	I'm sure we'll be able to sort this out to your satisfaction.
Guest	…

Unit 14: Group discussion and making a speech

This unit offers opportunities for group discussion and making speeches. You will practise expressing and supporting opinions, and using rhetorical devices.

1   In groups of three, study the photograph. What thoughts and feelings does it evoke? Talk about what you see and its implications.

2   Read the newspaper article on health, as preparation for a group discussion. Look up any words which you don't know.

138

In recent years we've all become more health conscious, but in doing so we seem to have perverted the meaning of health. Health is no longer something everyone is born with and retains if they are lucky. Health is a commodity. It is something you can have more of. And to qualify for this extra health you have to buy a tracksuit, eat vitamin pills, have a therapist and learn to do one-handed press-ups.

This all sounds quite harmless – until you realise it implies that people who are not perfectly formed, who are not young, sporty and sun-tanned, are less valuable people. We all want to be healthy, but we should perhaps come down off the exercise bike and clarify what the word health actually means.

For a start, health is not beauty and fitness. You can have wonderful hair and huge muscles, while your internal organs are in a terrible state. The outer person is not a direct reflection of the inner person. If life were that simple, medical diagnosis would be an awful lot easier.

Second, health is not a purely physical state. It's mental as well. There are lots of supremely fit people who are psychologically deranged and, conversely, a lot of quite seriously disabled people who are bright, happy and perfectly in tune with themselves. Compulsive slimming and exercising are a form of obsession – and obsession is a form of mental illness.

Besides, the criteria for physical and mental health are a matter of opinion, containing a strong social element. In any society except his own, Attila the Hun would have been regarded as a psychopath. There's a tribe in the Amazon rainforest which regards you as unwell if you don't have pale, circular patches of fungal infection on your skin.

Taking all this into account, health is a terribly difficult word to define. It is nevertheless important to do so, because unless we know what health is we don't know what to aim for. Enshrined in the constitution of the World Health Organization is this statement: 'Health is a state of complete physical, mental and social well-being, and not merely the absence of disease or infirmity.' Arguably, this says it all, but by this definition will there ever be a world in which we can say everyone is healthy?

My own favourite definition of health is 'psychological health is the ability to love and to work'. It's an easy thing to aim for and at the same time very difficult to arrive at. There are, however, occasional moments in everyone's life when you experience, simultaneously, a great love for those around you and also a great sense of personal fulfilment. These fleeting moments are very hard to achieve, but they constitute a more worthwhile aim in life than trying to look like a supermodel.

Adapted from an article by John Collee, *The Observer*.

TASK TIP

You need to be able to distinguish between fact and opinion in many kinds of speech and writing. Journalism mixes the two, and the more it uses opinion rather than fact, the more it is trying to manipulate the reader, and the less genuinely informative it is. Certain verbs help you to identify which is which, so that you can detect how much bias there is in a piece of writing or a speech:

- Facts tend to be introduced by *is, does, can, will, has, proves, shows*.
- Opinions tend to be introduced by *hopes, claims, thinks, believes, expects, accuses, suggests*.
- Vocabulary choice indicates the writer's viewpoint and bias; words with strong connotations likely to evoke an emotive reaction show approval or disapproval.

However, in the article in Activity **2** the verb *to be* is used throughout to apply to both facts and opinions, making it difficult for the reader to distinguish them. Notice the use of first and second person plural (*we* and *you*) in the article. Personal references and direct appeals are used in arguments to create a relationship with the reader, but they should be balanced by facts, statistics and dates to convey the impression of knowledge and objectivity. Exaggeration for conveying ridicule or creating humour can be an effective method of securing reader interest, sympathy and support, but this is further evidence of a biased attitude by the writer.

KEY POINT

The ideal number for a group is four or five; fewer limits the range of opinions and more makes it difficult for everyone to participate equally.

When taking part in group discussion, you should not dominate it by talking too much, or say so little that your views are not expressed. You must not interrupt other speakers or use aggressive language, and you should listen attentively to their views so that you can respond to them. The aim is to follow on from what the previous speaker has said by agreeing or disagreeing, and by adding a new fact or opinion to the discussion. The discussion should move on from its starting point and extend more widely – though still relevantly – to avoid repetition of the same ideas. Evidence to support your point of view will give it greater impact; you might cite statistics, media reports, or your own experience or that of someone you know.

3   Some of the statements in the article are facts; others are opinions. With your partner, find **five** examples of each and put them into two columns in note form. Examples have been provided.

Fact	Opinion
obsession is a form of mental illness	Health is a commodity

4   Discuss in groups of four or five your response to the article. Use some of the ideas below to help you structure the discussion.

- Agree on a title for the article which makes clear the writer's viewpoint.
- Come to an agreement on a definition of health which represents the views of your group.
- Discuss how biased you think the article is, giving specific evidence to support your conclusion.
- Say whether you think people generally are more or less healthy than they used to be.
- Express your view of the future of medicine.
- Say whether you think that disease can and should be eradicated.
- Discuss how attitudes to health have changed over time.
- Consider the state of hospitals, the health service and the medical profession in your country.
- Talk about your own state of health and fitness, and explain your attitude towards exercise.

139

5   Read the following article about a rock concert as preparation for a discussion.

WHY ARE ROCK FANS SO STUPID?

Imagine this scenario. Armed with a really expensive pair of tickets for the opera, you turn up with a quarter of an hour to spare. You queue up at the bar for a glass of white wine and then take your seat. Then you wait, and wait, and keep on waiting.

A slow handclap goes ignored, a few boos are drowned out with a CD and no one seems to care when a couple in the audience snatch up their coats and leave. Two hours later, the curtain lifts, the show starts and the crowd goes wild; everything is forgiven.

It is not just unlikely; it is unheard of. Angry punters would have stormed out and demanded a full refund. The media would have fulminated. But when it comes to rock concerts, it is exactly the sort of thing we put up with.

On Wednesday, a friend and I paid £90 each to see our childhood heroes, Guns N' Roses, at the Hammersmith Apollo in west London. The band were due on at 8.45 p.m. and it was meant to all be over in time for people to catch last trains.

That did not happen. We turned up a little late, grabbed some drinks and took our place – trapped in the middle of a group of fans – at just after nine. It was hot and dark. The floor was sticky, and every time people around me moved, my drink was spilt. But I was excited about the gig, so I put up with it.

Ten came and went and we became a little restless. 'Typical Axl Rose,' quipped one man about the lead singer. He hollered and booed to no avail. Another man said: 'I'm not putting up with this,' and stormed off. But most of us just waited, convinced they were about to run on stage. And as soon as they did (two hours late), the crowd went mad, screaming and cheering, and the man who had stomped off rushed back with a huge smile. It was a hot day, we were dehydrated and a bit dizzy, but we loved it.

Where else would you spend that much and then tolerate standing for two hours in a cramped space waiting for your evening's entertainment? If a football match due to start at 3 p.m. did not kick off until 5 p.m., organisers would expect to face the wrath of angry fans.

Yet, when it comes to bands, fans grin and bear it. If you had asked me on Thursday whether I enjoyed the gig the night before, I would have said it was amazing. When the crowd spilled out at 1 a.m., many having missed their last trains, they still looked happy.

For the cost of our tickets, we could have flown to Morocco, Turkey or Italy. I could have eaten in a Michelin-starred restaurant or bought a designer outfit.

But I persist in thinking it was worth every penny. In fact, given the chance again, I might even pay more than £90 to spend two uncomfortable hours waiting for Guns N' Roses.

So why are rock fans so stupid?

Adapted from 'Oh, the hell we rock fans put up with', by Anushka Asthana, www.guardian.co.uk, 11th June 2006.

During the discussion, you will be expected to give a point of view at the appropriate moment, and to support it. This is a sophisticated speaking skill, requiring you not only to consider content but also expression and tone of voice, so that you make your opinions clear without sounding extreme or disrespectful. Avoid emphatic adverbs – such as *obviously*, *totally*, *utterly* – as they will make you sound dogmatic and unwilling to consider views different from your own.

Remember that your listening as well as your speaking skills need to be developed. A good listener responds appropriately to the contributions of others and treats other members of the group as equals. Aim to argue persuasively but not aggressively; act confidently as group leader when necessary; refer back to previous points; move the discussion forward; listen without interrupting; consider the views of others.

6 In groups, hold a discussion, which your teacher may assess, taking the article in Activity **5** as a starting point. Express your views about the behaviour of the fans in the passage, and then move on to the idea of fanaticism generally.

As you speak and listen, think about which comments being made in the discussion are facts and which are only opinions, and respond appropriately.

- What are the characteristics of a fan?
- What kinds of pursuits attract fans?
- What are you a fan of, and how did you become one?
- What are the attractions/benefits of being a fan?
- What makes someone become a fanatic?
- What are the dangers of fanaticism?

7 Practise making short speeches, of about 100 words each. Choose one or more topics from the list below, plan in your head what you are going to say, then tell the rest of the class your opinion.

The most enjoyable food

141

The perfect holiday

The ideal friend

The most entertaining television programme

The best day of the week

8 You and your partner disagree completely! One of you will argue for and the other will argue against one of the moral dilemmas listed below. The class will vote on who makes the more convincing speech in each pair.

Your teacher will tell you which one to prepare and deliver. Begin either *Yes, because …* or *No, because …*

a You know your friend has cheated in their coursework by downloading a composition from the Internet. Do you tell anyone about your discovery?

b You knock over and break an ornament at a relative's house. Do you blame the cat?

c You are given too much change for a purchase in a shop. Do you tell the assistant and return the extra money?

d You caused slight damage to a parked car with your bicycle. Do you leave a note with your name and address?

e You see someone shoplifting whom you know slightly. Do you tell the shop owner?

f Your parents think you did well in recent school exams because there was a mistake in the grade on the report. Do you tell them the truth?

g It is possible for you to pay less than you should for a train journey by lying about which station you came from. Do you?

h You find a wallet in the street containing some money and an address. Do you contact the owner?

i You did not do your homework because you went out with your friends instead. Do you tell your teacher the real reason for not doing it?

j You try on a new garment when you get home from the shop and you spill something on it. Do you take it back and ask for a free replacement, claiming that the stain was already there?

9   Imagine you are a famous real person, dead or alive, male or female. You are in a hot-air balloon over the Himalayas with other famous people. The balloon is losing height and descending rapidly towards the snowy peaks. Some of you have to be thrown out in order for the balloon to rise again and for the rest to be saved. The quality of your argument will be a matter of life and death!

Your teacher will allocate roles and you need to think about what kind of person you are (for example, politician, artist, composer, writer, scientist, pop star, film star, philanthropist, inventor) and why you are of value to the human race.

a   You have only two minutes to jot down some notes.

b   One by one around the class, argue why you should stay in the basket. You have three minutes of speaking time to justify your past, present and future existence. The teacher will decide whether or not to throw you out on the basis of how persuasive your speech is.

TASK TIP

Although most formal speaking is planned, scripted, rehearsed and/or aided by notes, the delivery of a speech should sound spontaneous and authentic. Written prompts should therefore be as discreet as possible.

Look at your audience while you are speaking; everyone knows that newsreaders and politicians read from an autocue – and may not have written their own speeches anyway – but these public speakers keep eye contact with the audience as a way of winning trust.

Bear in mind that three minutes is a long time when speaking uninterrupted, and needs a surprising amount of material for normal speaking speed.

10 Listen to the extract below being read aloud, then discuss as a class what impression the speech has made on you. Did you notice any use of rhetoric? Which words/phrases do you remember?

This is a short extract from Nelson Mandela's statement at Pretoria Supreme Court on April 20 1964, made at the opening of the defence case in the Rivonia trial.

I am prepared to die

[...] Africans want to be paid a living wage. Africans want to perform work which they are capable of doing, and not work which the government declares them to be capable of. We want to be allowed to live where we obtain work, and not be endorsed out of an area because we were not born there. We want to be allowed to own land in places where we work, and not to be obliged to live in rented houses which we can never call our own. We want to be part of the general population, and not confined to living in our ghettoes. African men want to have their wives and children to live with them where they work, and not be forced into an unnatural existence in men's hostels. Our women want to be with their menfolk and not be left permanently widowed in the reserves. We want to be allowed out after eleven o'clock at night and not to be confined to their rooms like little children. We want to be allowed to travel in our own country and to seek work where we want to and not where the Labour Bureau tells us to. We want a just share in the whole of South Africa; we want security and a stake in society.

Above all, My Lord, we want equal political rights, because without them our disabilities will be permanent. I know this sounds revolutionary to the whites in this country, because the majority of voters will be Africans. This makes the white man fear democracy.

But this fear cannot be allowed to stand in the way of the only solution which will guarantee racial harmony and freedom for all. It is not true that the enfranchisement of all will result in racial domination. Political division, based on colour, is entirely artificial and, when it disappears, so will the domination of one colour group by another. The ANC has spent half a century fighting against racialism. When it triumphs as certainly it must, it will not change that policy.

This then is what the ANC is fighting for. Our struggle is a truly national one. It is a struggle of the African people, inspired by our own suffering and our own experience. It is a struggle for the right to live.

During my lifetime I have dedicated myself to this struggle of the African people. I have fought against white domination, and I have fought against black domination. I have cherished the ideal of a democratic and free society in which all persons live together in harmony and with equal opportunities. It is an ideal which I hope to live for and to see realised. But, My Lord, if needs be, it is an ideal for which I am prepared to die.

11 Now look at the text. With a partner, find the rhetorical devices of structure, and vocabulary. List the devices you have found and describe how they are effective.

> **TASK TIP**
>
> When making public speeches of any kind, whether in school meetings or national parliaments, speakers use rhetorical devices to make their message more emphatic, more memorable, more emotive – and therefore more persuasive. The typical devices, which mostly belong in pairs, are:
>
> - repetition/tautology (saying it again in the same words or in other words)
> - euphemism/provocation (finding less or more shocking ways of saying something)
> - hyperbole/meiosis/litotes (exaggerating or minimising a situation or statistic)
> - doubles/triples (using grammar structures in groups of two or three)
> - pathos/bathos (evoking pity or ridicule in the listener)
> - oxymoron/paradox (a literal or conceptual contradiction)
> - irony/satire/sarcasm (pointing out an absurdity or mocking someone or something; saying the opposite of what you mean for effect)
> - juxtaposition (putting two ideas together to imply a link between them).

12 If you were directing this speech to be delivered in a film, what instructions would you give the actor playing Nelson Mandela? With your partner, decide where and how the actor should include the following:

a pauses

b tone and volume changes

c pace changes

d emphasis on certain words

e body language.

13 Write your own speech about a social, political or intellectual issue which really matters to you (e.g. animal rights, universal peace or free education for all). Make it about 500 words long. (This can be used as a coursework assignment.) Record your speech.

Your teacher will play everyone's speech back to the class. Refer to the band descriptors for your examination syllabus and decide what mark you would give each speech, and why.

KEY POINT

The first considerations when preparing a public speech are:

- Aim – What is the goal? (What is it you need to convince the audience of?)
- Audience – Who are they? (How many of them are there? Why are they there? How much do they already know? What are their expectations?)
- Context – How much time do you have? How formal is the occasion? Is humour appropriate? Can visual aids be used?

The next three aspects to be considered are:

- Content – Select strong points, enough but not too many; make them interesting, relevant, supported and ordered; develop each idea but without spending too long on it.
- Style – Use precise and evocative words, not those meant simply to impress; use devices to make you sound well informed and passionate about the issue, but not over-emotional.
- Delivery – Speak more slowly than you normally would; vary pace and tone of voice; think about timing/pausing.

14 Your class is going to hold a formal debate. Your teacher will assess everyone's contribution as a speaker and as a listener.

Follow the procedure below.

a As a class discuss and decide on a motion (subject for the debate). Your teacher writes the motion on the board in the form *This house believes that …*

b The class divides into four groups, with three or four students in each. (If the class is larger than 16 students, make six groups.) Half are told they are to speak for the motion (proposers), the other half against (opposers).

c Each group elects a speaker to deliver the group's contribution to the debate. The speaker collects and records the ideas of everyone in the group in note form. Remember, it doesn't matter whether you personally agree with the side you are presenting.

d The group selects the best points and finds support for them, with statistics for example. It is a good idea to try to predict the points the other side will make so that you can counteract them. The group agrees on the best order for the points.

e The elected speaker rehearses the speech quietly to his or her own group, and as a result improves it stylistically and structurally, and adjusts the length. Formal language is used in debate speeches, which begin *Ladies and gentlemen …*

f The debate is conducted, with the teacher as chair, in this order: first proposer, first opposer, second proposer, second opposer, and so on.

g While the rest of the class – the 'floor' – listen, they are assessing the quality of the arguments and thinking of possible questions to ask when all the speeches have been delivered.

h The chair asks if there are any questions from the floor. You can ask the relevant speaker for clarification of a point or challenge his or her claims with a counter point or contradictory evidence. The speaker responds briefly to your questions and challenges.

i The chair calls for votes for the motion, votes against the motion and abstentions. You should vote according to the quality of the arguments and delivery, not according to your own views or friendships. Only abstain if you think both sides are equal. The teacher counts hands and announces the result of the debate.

➕ Further practice

a Listen to a political debate, or an extract from one, on radio or television. This could be a parliamentary broadcast or an argument between guests on a news programme. List all the rhetorical devices you can identify, think about how they were intended to influence the audience, and judge the effectiveness of the speeches.

b Script an argument dialogue, of about 500 words (this could be used for a coursework assignment), between two speakers who believe strongly for and against a controversial issue. Use A and B in the margin to identify the speakers, and give a balanced and comprehensive argument covering both sides. Use strong and emotive language, as well as some of the rhetorical devices you have learned about.

c Below is an example of urban graffiti. Some people find it attractive and believe it serves a useful purpose, others believe it is ugly and criminal.

   i Write points, in two columns, for both sides of a discussion on the topic of graffiti.

   ii Choose which side to argue, then write a speech of about 500 words (which could be used for a coursework assignment) in which you refute the other point of view and then strongly present your case, using supporting evidence.

List of terms

abbreviation shortened form of a word, e.g. *Dr*

acronym series of initials (which may form a kind of word, e.g. WYSIWYG) that stand for a much longer group of words

alliteration repetition of the initial letter in adjacent words, e.g. *dark dank dungeon*

antithesis words balanced to create contrast

argumentative designed to convince reader to accept a particular view

assonance repetition of the vowel sound in neighbouring words, e.g. *deep sleep*

autobiography account of a person's life written by him/herself

biography account of a person's life written by someone else

blurb publisher's brief description of a book, printed on the back cover

brainstorm immediate thoughts and associations for a particular topic

brochure pamphlet containing illustrations and information about a product or service

chronological arrangement of events in order in which they occurred

clause group of words containing a **finite verb**

cliché well-known and overused phrase, e.g. *Once upon a time*

climax point of greatest intensity in a narrative text

collate collect and combine information from two or more sources

colloquialisms everyday spoken language

complex sentence sentence consisting of one main clause and one or more **subordinate clauses**, e.g. *After he had supper, he went to bed.*

compound sentence sentence formed from two **simple sentences** using *and*, *but*, *so* or *or*, e.g. *He ate supper and he went to bed.*

connective joining word used to form compound or complex sentences, e.g. *but*, *although*, *since*

connotation additional implied meaning of a word

context surrounding parts or setting of a text

description attempt to enable the reader to visualise something

dialogue spoken words between two people; direct speech between several people used in a narrative or drama text

direct speech speech reproduced exactly as it was spoken, in inverted commas

discourse markers adverbials at the start of a paragraph which indicate the progression of the discussion

discursive discusses something informatively from different viewpoints

editorial newspaper or magazine editor's published comment on a topical issue

embedded clause type of subordinate relative clause introduced by who or what, without being preceded by a comma as it defines and belongs with the subject

empathy ability to identify with the experience and feelings of someone else

euphemism tactful or evasive way of referring to something controversial or distasteful, e.g. *passed away, ethnic cleansing*

evoke call up a response

explicit stated clearly

figurative non-literal use of language

finite verb verb that has a subject

flyer leaflet distributed to advertise an event or product

genre category of speech or writing, e.g. **narrative**

gist main ideas contained in a text or speech

imagery pictures created in words: see **simile** and **metaphor**

imaginative fictional or subjective

implicit implied, though not overtly expressed

imperative verb form of the verb that makes a direct request or gives an order, e.g. *Please be quiet.*

inference deduction or conclusion that can be drawn from a text

informative transactional text containing data

149

intensifier adverb without meaning which indicates strength of following word, e.g. *really amazing, very soon*

jargon specialised or technical language of a profession or other related group that is difficult for others to understand

logo sign representing an organisation or company

main clause principal clause of a **complex sentence**, which can be a sentence in its own right, e.g. *After he had supper,* <u>*he went to bed*</u>.

metaphor comparison without using *as* or *like* which uses one or more words in a **figurative** way, e.g. *The ship* <u>*ploughed*</u> *through the waves.*

mind map diagram for visualising links between ideas and information

mnemonic technique for remembering something

monologue speech by one person

mood feelings evoked in a reader by a narrative or descriptive text

narrative tells a story; consists of **plot** and character

non-fiction believed to be true

nuance subtle meaning

obituary summary of and praise for a famous person's life, published on their death

onomatopoeia word that sounds like its meaning, e.g. *rustling*

paraphrase express the same meaning in different words

parenthesis grammatically non-essential part of a sentence, indicated by a pair of punctuation marks

participle part of a verb which can be used independently as an adjective; may be present, e.g. *shining*, or past, e.g. *damaged*

pathos pity or sorrow created for a fictional character or real person

personification giving human attributes to non-human things

phonetic relating to sound

phrase group of words that does not contain a **finite verb**, e.g. after *eating his supper*

plagiarism stealing the expression of another writer and presenting it as one's own

plot events in a **narrative**

prefix letter(s) added to the beginning of a word to alter its meaning, e.g. <u>*un*</u>*happy*

propaganda text or speech attempting to persuade others to adopt a particular political or religious viewpoint; exaggerated and selective version of events

register level of formality or particular style of expression, shaped by context

reported speech speech that is reproduced indirectly, without inverted commas

rhetoric language features designed to persuade

scan read a text to identify specific information

simile comparison using as or *like*, e.g. *She was like a fish out of water.*

simple sentence sentence consisting of a single **main clause**, e.g. *He went to bed.*

skim read a text quickly to grasp its **gist**

standard English form of English without regional variations of grammar which can be understood by all users of the language

stem part of a word that has its own meaning, e.g. *dyno, aero*, to which **prefixes** or **suffixes** can be attached

structure order and organisation of content of a text or speech

style selection and organisation of language elements

subordinate clause clause of a **complex sentence**, generally introduced by a **connective**, which cannot stand as a sentence on its own, e.g. <u>*After he had supper,*</u> he went to bed.

suffix letter(s) added to the end of an existing word to alter its form or meaning, e.g. *manage*<u>*ment*</u>

summarise reduce a text to its essential ideas

superlative adjective ending in *est* or preceded by *most* to indicate the highest degree

synonym word/phrase with similar meaning to another

synopsis brief summary or outline of a plot

syntax grammatical arrangement of words and phrases to form sentences

Acknowledgements

The author and publishers are grateful for the permission to reproduce texts in either the original or adapted form. While every effort has been made, it has not always been possible to identify the sources of all the materials used, or to trace all copyright holders. If any omissions are brought to our notice, we will be happy to include the appropriate acknowledgements on reprinting.

p. 4 'Cape Town' reproduced by permission of SA-Venues.com

p. 5 *Pole to Pole* by Michael Palin, published by Weidenfeld and Nicholson, an imprint of The Orion Publishing Group, London. Copyright © Michael Palin, 1995.

p. 10 'The big chill' (Walter Ellis), Sunday Times, November 2000.

p.14 'A rock and a hard place' (Peter and Leni Gillman), Sunday Times, December 1995. Copyright © Peter Gillman.

p. 16 Logo and text used by permission of the Duke of Edinburgh's Award International Association.

p. 17 'White water action in Victoria Falls' reproduced by permission of Shearwater Victoria Falls, www.shearwatervictoriafalls.com

p. 22 From *Life of Pi* by Yann Martel (Harcourt, 2001). Copyright © 2001 Yann Martel. With permission of the author.

p.22 Extract from *Life of Pi* by Yann Martel, reproduced by permission of Canongate, Random House of Canada Ltd.

p.24 Extract from *My Family and other Animals* by Gerald Durrell reproduced by permission of Curtis Brown Group Ltd, London on behalf of the estate of Gerald Durrell. Copyright © Gerald Durrell 1956.

p.32 'Internet Global Leader' used with kind permission of Tom Hadfield.

p. 37 'Why the old woman limps', Lupenga Mphande used by kind permission of the author.

p. 38 'The *Africa Mercy*", by Dan McDougall used by kind permission of the author.

p. 44 'Rescuers Find Trapped Student Cavers Alive', by Charles Bremner, The Times, 19th May 2001. © The Times/NI Syndication.

p. 47 ABCNEWS VideoSource

p. 51 Extract from *The Road from Coorain: An Australian Memoir* by Jill Ker Conway, 1989, published by William Heinemann Ltd. Reprinted by permission of the Random House Group Ltd.

p.60 Biography from the official Roald Dahl website www.roalddahl.com, by permission of David Higham Associates on behalf of the author's estate.

p 62 Used with permission of The Associated Press Copyright © 2009. All rights reserved.

p. 63 'His life was cloaked in myth and legend' (Simon Sebag Montifore), Sunday Times, March 2000. © The Times/NI Syndication.

p.72 'The joys of jogging' (Emily Wilson), Guardian, September 2000. Copyright Guardian News & Media Ltd. 2000.

p.74 'Great news, Dad, now I'm 16 the law says I can drive', Dominic Tobin, Sunday Times, 20th January 2013. © The Times/NI syndication.

p. 76 From *Tales from Firozsha Baag* (Penguin Books Canada, 1987, McClelland & Stewart, 1992, 1997). Copyright © 1987 Rohinton Mistry. With permission of the author.

p. 83 From *The Woman in Black* by Susan Hill, published by Vintage 1983, reproduced by permission of Sheil Land Associates Ltd. © Susan Hill 1983.

p. 84 Extract from 'The Wasteland' reprinted with the permission of Scribner Publishing Group, a Division of Simon & Schuster, Inc., from *Tales from a Troubled Land* by Alan Paton. Copyright © 1961 by Alan Paton. Copyright renewed © 1989 by Anne Paton. All rights reserved. "The Wasteland" by Alan Paton from *Tales from a Troubled Land*. Publisher Charles Scribner's Sons, New York, 1959. With permission from Alan Paton Will Trust.

p. 85 Extract from 'The Green Mamba' in *Going Solo*, by Roald Dahl, published by Penguin 1986, by permission of David Higham Associates on behalf of the author's estate.

p. 87 'Stopping by woods on a snowy evening', by Robert Frost. With permission from Henry Holt and Co. LLC and Random House, UK.

p. 95 'One man and his sub' (Nicholas Brautlect), Sunday Times, February 2001. With kind permission of the author.

p. 107 The Lakewood Scoop. TheLakewoodScoop.com

p. 108 Adapted from an article by Simon Trump and Tim Robbins, Sunday Times, June 2001 © The Times/NI Syndication and author.

p. 112 'Text-talk teens lack the right words for work' by Sian Griffiths and Chris Gourlay, Sunday Times, January, 2010. © The Times/NI Syndication.

p. 112 Caroline Grant, 'How predictive texting takes its toll on a child's brain', Mail Online, 11 August, 2009. © Daily Mail.

p. 118 Used with kind permission of Chris Rose.

p. 123 Extract from 'The Hitch-hiker' by Roald Dahl, published by Jonathon Cape 1977, by permission of David Higham Associates.

p. 138 (John Collee), 'The real meaning of health', Observer, 30/12/1990. Copyright Guardian News & Media Ltd. 1990.

p. 140 'Oh the hell we rock fans put up with' (Anushka Asthana), Observer, June 2006. Copyright Guardian News & Media Ltd. 2006.

p. 144 With kind permission from the Nelson Mandela Foundation.

The publishers would like to thank the following for permission to reproduce photographs:

p. 1 feiyuezhangjie/Shutterstock; p. 3 Pawel Kazmierczak/Shutterstock; p. 4 michseljung/Shutterstock; p.5 WitR/Shutterstock; p. 6 Steve White-Thomson; p. 8 www.wikipaintings.org/en/n-c-wyeth/robinson-crusoe-illustration; p. 10 Volodymyr Goinyk/Shutterstock; p. 11 http://en.wikipedia.org/wiki/Last_voyage_of_the_Karluk; p. 12 staphy/Dreamstime; p. 13 bambuh/Shutterstock; p. 13 RM/Alamy; p. 14 Greg Epperson/Shutterstock; p. 15 Patrick Poendl/Shutterstock; p. 16 www.intaward.org/; p. 17 Ammit Jack/Shutterstock; p. 17 Paul Keller/Shutterstock; p. 17 Jay Bo/Shutterstock; p. 19 Dennis van der Water/Shutterstock; p. 21 yuris/Shutterstock; p.22 rujithal/Shutterstock; p. 23 abc7/Shutterstock; p. 23 Naturefriend/Dreamstime; p. 24 Olympus/Shutterstock; p. 24 Danny Xu/Shutterstock; p. 25 Eric Isselee/Shutterstock; p. 26 Kzenon/Shutterstock; p. 27 Ollyy/Shutterstock; p. 27 p. 28 Olavs/Shutterstock; p. 28 testing/Shutterstock; p. 29 Krishna.Wu/Shutterstock; p.30 Eat/Shutterstock; p. 31 Syaheir Azizan/Shutterstock; p. 32 Tom Hadfield; p. 33 martan/Shutterstock; p. 34 emei/Shutterstock; p. 36 nelik/Shutterstock; p. 37 Danita Delimont/Alamy; p. 38 www.mercyships.org.uk/africa-mercy; p. 41 Lesya Dolyuk/Shutterstock; p. 43 http://arkvillhistory.blogspot.co.uk/2012/07/the-memories-of-edith-colman-part-1.html; p. 44 DSdesign/Shutterstock; p. 46 Joggie Botma/Shutterstock; p. 47 © Press Association Images; p. 47 ievgen sosnytskyi /Shutterstock; p. 48 robin2/Shutterstock; p. 48. ducu59us/Shutterstock; p. 49 nuttakit/Shutterstock; p. 50 © Tasmanian Conservation Trust; p. 51 © Press Association; p. 52 Tatkuptsova/Dreamstime; p. 53 Bill Bachmann/age fotostock/ SuperStock: p. 55 http://en.wikipedia.org/wiki/Mary_Celeste: p. 55 © PhotoStock-Israel/Alamy; p. 56 Gelpi JM/Shutterstock; p. 58 Tupungato/Shutterstock; p. 59 stocksolutions/Shutterstock; p. 59 http://commons.wikimedia.org/wiki/File:Zeinab_Badawi_crop_AIB.jpg; p. 60 Warner Bros./Kobal Collection/Peter Mountain/images.de; p. 62 Jorge Hackerman/Shutterstock; p. 63 Mary Evans Picture Library/Alamy; p. 65 Popova Valeriya/Shutterstock; p. 66 © Kobal Collection; p. 67 S. Papadopoulos/Robert Harding; p. 68 motorolka/Shutterstock; p. 69 vasabil/Shutterstock; p. 70 margouillat photo/Shutterstock; p. 72 Boguslaw Mazur/Shutterstock; Szefei/Dreamstime; p. 72 zeber/Shutterstock; p. 74 wavebreakmedia/Shutterstock; p. 74 ElenaShow/Shutterstock; p. 77 Bryan Sikora/Shutterstock; p. 77 Christos Georghiou/Shutterstock; p. 78 Horizons WWP/Alamy: p. 81 Mirenska Olga/Shutterstock; p.83 phoelix/Shutterstock; p. 84 MitarArt/Shutterstock; p.87 Romiana Lee/Shutterstock; p. 88 Denys Prykhodov/Shutterstock; p. 89 somchai rakin/Shutterstock; p. 91 Narit Jindajamorn/Shutterstock; p. 93 Monkey Business Images/Shutterstock; p.94 Antonio Guillem/Shutterstock; p. 96 Maxim Gargulin/Shutterstock; p. 98 Irkusnya/Dreamstime; p. 98 Jultud/Dreamstime; p. 99 Jan Willem van Hofwegen/Shutterstock; p. 101 meunierd/Shutterstock; p. 104 AlanJeffery/Dreamstime; p. 106 Roughcollie/Dreamstime; p. 107 Mircea Costina/Dreamstime; p. 109 Dirk Ecken/Shutterstock; p. 111 OLJ Studio/Shutterstock; p. 112 Singkham/Shutterstock; p. 115 Sergiu Turcanu/Alamy; p. 122 Djomas/Shutterstock; p. 123 Solovyova Lyudmyla/Shutterstock; p. 125 ansem/Shutterstock; p. 127 © Getty Images; p. 128 Daneilal/Dreamstime; p. 129 Jacek Chabraszewski/Shutterstock; p. 130 Teguh Mujono/Shutterstock; pp. 130-1 pking4th/Shutterstock; p. 136 Michael D Brown/Shutterstock; p. 136. Jan Hyman/Shutterstock; p. 136 HuHu/Shutterstock; p. 136. OK-SANA/Shutterstock; p. 137 bilderlounge/Getty; p. 138 © Press Association; p. 138 bikeriderlondon/Shutterstock; p. 140 Franz Pflug/Dreamstime; p. 141 MaraZe/Shutterstock; p. 141 John Warner/Shutterstock; p. 142 Ashusha/Shutterstock; p. 146 Negovura/Shutterstock; p. 146 Frantisek Czanner/Shutterstock; p. 147 Daj/Getty; p. 148 Banana Republic Images/Shutterstock

Cover image: Shutterstock © Jo Crebbin

 Produced for Cambridge University Press by White-Thomson Publishing +44 (0)843 208 7460 www.wtpub.co.uk

Project editor: Lyn Ward
Designer: Ian Winton
Illustrators: Chabluk Illustration and Steve Evans Illustration